Jumpstart Jamstack Development

Build and deploy modern websites and web apps
using Gatsby, Netlify, and Sanity

Christopher Pecoraro

Vincenzo Gambino

BIRMINGHAM—MUMBAI

Jumpstart Jamstack Development

Group Product Manager: Ashwin Nair
Publishing Product Manager: Ashitosh Gupta
Senior Editor: Sofi Rogers
Content Development Editor: Abhishek Jadhav
Technical Editor: Shubham Sharma
Copy Editor: Safis Editing
Project Coordinator: Manthan Patel
Proofreader: Safis Editing
Indexer: Priyanka Dhadke
Production Designer: Roshan Kawale

First published: May 2021
Production reference: 1070521

Published by Packt Publishing Ltd.
Livery Place
35 Livery Street
Birmingham
B3 2PB, UK.

ISBN 978-1-80020-349-5

www.packt.com

This book is written in honor and loving memory of my father

Dr. George Anthony Pecoraro, Sr.

He gave his all for us

and also in memory of my friend

Nicholas Robert Pinansky עבשילא'ו דוד רב לאונמע

and my dear cousins

Sergeant Gregory Lee Smith

and

Airman First Class Victor Joseph Guida

Questo libro è stato scritto in memoria del Professor Ingegnere Serafino Casu.

È stato per me come un padre.

I would like to especially thank my wife, Dr. Anna Casu, sa prenda mea, for her divine patience, spousal love, and eternal support, together with my mother, Patricia Marie Pecoraro, for her selfless and indescribable love. Thanks to my family, both in the United States and Italy. Appreciation goes to my educators Br. David Carlson OSB, Dr. Colleen Carr, and Dr. Harold Morrison at Saint Vincent College.

I would like to thank Luke Woodling, Cliff Manspeaker, Clinton J Robinson, Logo Olagoke, and all of my other colleagues at Rollins College.

Also, special thanks go to Aaron LeClair for believing in me, and Harmony Betancourt, Efrain Lugo, and Nick Clements for their continued encouragement and friendship.

To my former colleagues: Geoffrey Bent, Steven Dudukovich, Nate See, Shen DeShayne, and so many others that I have unfortunately forgotten.

Thanks to Sanity: Magnus for liking my tweet that inspired this book, and Knut, Kapehe, and Bryan for continued support throughout the writing process.

Last and certainly not least, GRAZIE to my coauthor Vincenzo, and Silvia and Thea.

We sadly remember those who have lost their lives during the COVID-19 pandemic and honor those who gave everything to defeat it.

– Christopher Pecoraro

To my beloved wife, Silvia, whose strength and determination inspire me. You are and always will be my perfect wife and mother to our children. I really love you and I mean you.

To my "sleeping on a dandelion" daughter, Thea Sofia: choose your own ground and follow your dreams.

To my mother Anna Maria, my father Giuseppe, and my sister Alice, with love and gratitude.

To my niece Emma and nephews Massimiliano, Alessandro P., Gabriele, and Alessandro S., who always make me smile.

In memory of my grandparents Rocco Battaglia, Angela Cardinale, Vincenzo Gambino, and Rosalia Bronzino.

To my coauthor and friend, Christopher Pecoraro, who supported me in my programming career.

– Vincenzo Gambino

Foreword

Innovation is often driven by people who expect more and challenge the status quo. Instead of making small improvements to what is, they invent new paths that over time become inevitable. We reach a point where we can't imagine going back to where we came from.

The most common solutions for building web pages today were created in the early 2000s. What was once state of the art is now limiting digital projects and content collaboration, frustrating developers and content editors and leaving product and business owners with infrastructure that creates poor digital customer experiences and harms their capacity for digital transformation.

We are now finally seeing a reinvention of the way we approach content and digital experiences on the web, and the frameworks and services commonly known as Jamstack are a big part of this revolution. They have emerged as a response to the constraints of traditional monolithic web architectures: organizations need more security, scalability, and to service their audience's demand for better content at an ever-increasing rate of delivery.

Jamstack fulfills these needs in ways that monolithic systems simply cannot. These tools are redefining what's possible on the web – and this book is the primer you need to make the leap into this new way of building. Christopher Pecoraro and Vincenzo Gambino provide a step-by-step process for building your own blazing-fast website and real-time backend by combining three innovative and industry-leading tools:

- **GatsbyJS**: the highly popular React-based static site generator
- **Netlify**: the industry-leading Jamstack web host and content delivery network
- **Sanity.io**: the real-time content platform that lets you treat content as data

In addition to making fast websites, this book shows you how these tools can be used to present content to any application or device, as exemplified by powering an Amazon Alexa skill from the same content that drives your website.

This is the true promise of the tools you are introduced to in this book – they're capable of so much more than websites. This API-enabled constellation of microservices, structured content, and serverless computing also supports a higher goal of content velocity. Forward-thinking teams are embracing the fact that great websites are just the first step towards running unified content projects. They're ushering in a new way of working – where product and marketing content and workflows converge around a single source of truth, and shipping amazing omnichannel experiences is no longer a pipedream.

Since you are reading this book, you're probably a person who expects more, challenges the status quo, and the one who explores the bleeding edge. Together we are creating a paradigm shift, not only on how the web is built, but in the approach we take to content, and to building digital experiences at large.

See you on the other side...

Magnus Kongsli Hillestad

CEO @ Sanity.io

Contributors

About the authors

Christopher Pecoraro has been a senior software developer, speaker, and open source enthusiast since 1999 with experience in software development with a focus on web applications, apps, and content management systems.

Vincenzo Gambino has been a software developer since 2007. He started in Palermo, Italy, and is now based in London, UK. He has developed software and web applications for government departments and many educational entities, including one of the major universities in the United Kingdom. He is focused on web applications, virtual assistant apps, and content management systems.

About the reviewers

Nirmalya Ghosh is an experienced developer who has designed and developed complex applications from scratch. He also has experience building and managing teams and likes working with React and GraphQL.

Table of Contents

Preface

1

History of the Jamstack

The evolution of the Jamstack	2	The Jamstack acronym explained	7
HTML	2	Jamstack advantages	7
Server-side includes	3		
The Common Gateway Interface	3	Our Jamstack	9
Forms	4	GatsbyJS	9
Web page preprocessors	4	Sanity.io	9
Content Management Systems	4	Netlify	9
WordPress	5		
Ajax	5	Getting started with the Jamstack	9
JavaScript frameworks	5	Installation	10
The rise of the cloud	5	Prerequisites	10
High-speed access	6		
		Summary	11
The rise of the Jamstack	6		

2

Introduction to Sanity

Technical requirements	14	Introducing Sanity Manage	19
Account setup	14	Sanity.io project pages	19
Introduction to Sanity.io	14		
What is GROQ?	15	Sanity Studio overview	22
		Navigation	22
Creating a project	15	Summary	25

3

Exploring Sanity Studio

Technical requirements   27
Modifying the example author   28
Modifying the existing author   28
Creating an additional author   30

Removing and adding articles   32
Removing example articles   32

Creating a new article   33

Modifying the website settings and redeploying the website   35
Setting the website name   36
Redeployment through Netlify   37

Summary   38

4

Sanity Configuration and Schemas

Technical requirements   40
Modeling content with schemas   40
Cloning the project   40
Exploring the project's folders   42

Schema relationships   46
A one-to-one relationship   46
A one-to-many relationship   48

Extending, modifying, and deploying the schema   49
The event schema   49
The venue schema   50
The schema file   52
Deploying the schema   52

Summary   56

5

Sanity's GROQ Language

Technical requirements   58
Why GROQ?   58
Installing Vision   59

GROQ versus SQL   60
Basic queries with GROQ   62
Selecting all events   62
Selecting all upcoming events   63
Selecting all past events   64
Selecting upcoming virtual conference

and non-virtual conferences   64
Selecting specific event fields   64
Selecting specific fields from relationships   65

Advanced GROQ   66
Getting events by venues   66
Formatting the response   67
Count result   67

Summary   68

6
Sanity's GraphQL Playground

Technical requirements   69
An introduction to GraphQL   70
Deploying the GraphQL API   71
Basic GraphQL syntax   71

GROQ versus GraphQL   73

GraphQL playground basics   76
Query parameters   78

Summary   80

7
Gatsby – An Introduction

Technical requirements   82
Gatsby, built on React   82
Gatsby basic project structure   82
gatsby-config.js   83
dotenv   86

Key Gatsby files   87
Gatsby folders   88

The gatsby develop command   89
Summary   90

8
Gatsby and GraphQL

Technical requirements   91
GraphQL in GatsbyJS   92

GraphiQL, a GraphQL navigator   94
Summary   100

9
Gatsby Source Plugins

Technical Requirements   101
Understanding plugins   102
Node Package Manager   102
Semantic versioning   103
Installing a package from npm   103

Searching, installing, and
configuring plugins   106
The Gatsby Plugin Library   106

Searching for a plugin   108
Installing and configuring the
gatsby-source-filesystem plugin   109
Installing and configuring the gatsby-
transformer-remark plugin   112
Installing and configuring the
gatsby-source-drupal plugin   116

Summary   120
Further reading   121

10
Building Gatsby Components

Technical requirements	124	Gatsby page components	125
React components	124	Gatsby template components	126
Tag convention	124	Gatsby partial components	132
Understanding the types of components	124	Summary	134

11
APIs – Extending Gatsby

Technical requirements	135	Configuring a token form in Sanity	142
Introduction to APIs	136	Configuring a Netlify function	146
Gatsby – APIs	136	Summary	151
Creating a Netlify form	137		

12
APIs – Alexa Skills

Technical requirements	153	Configuring the skill through the skill interface	158
Alexa skill life cycle	154	Build	159
Skill interface	154	Code	168
Skill service	154	Test	179
Creating the skill	154	Summary	180

13
Tying It All Together

Technical requirements	181	Using the Tailwind CSS framework	183
Gatsby.js layout modifications	182	Improving and formatting the event list	186
Introducing Tailwind CSS	182	Preparing for deployment	187
Installing the Tailwind CSS framework	182	Cleaning up the code	188

Toggling the venue visibility 190   **Summary** 191

14
Deployment Using Netlify and Azure

Technical requirements	194	Netlify deployment via the	
Introduction to Netlify	194	command line	200
Netlify plugins	196	**Azure Static Web Apps**	
HTML Minify	196	**deployment**	201
		Static web app creation	202
Advanced configuration		Static web app continuous deployment	206
through the netlify.toml file	198		
		Summary	209

15
Conclusion

Summary of concepts	211	projects	216
The Jamstack's future	212	Contributing to Sanity	216
Jamstack, JAMstack, and JAM Stack	212	Contributing to Gatsby	219
		Contributing to Netlify	220
The Jamstack community			
resources	214	**Final thoughts**	220
Contributing to Jamstack		**Why subscribe?**	221

Other Books You May Enjoy

Index

Preface

The **Jamstack (JavaScript, API, and Markup)** enables web developers to create and publish modern and maintainable websites and web apps focused on speed, security, and accessibility by using tools such as Gatsby, Sanity, and Netlify. Developers working with the Jamstack will be able to put their knowledge to good use with this practical guide to static site generation and content management. This Jamstack book takes a hands-on approach to implementation and related methodologies that will have you up and running with modern web development in no time.

Complete with step-by-step explanations of essential concepts, practical examples, and self-assessment questions, you'll begin by building an event and venue schema structure, and then expand the functionality, exploring all that Jamstack has to offer. You'll learn how an example Jamstack is built, build structured content using a schema, use GraphQL to expose the content, and employ Gatsby to build an event website using page and template components. Lastly, you'll deploy the website to a Netlify server.

By the end of this book, you'll have gained the knowledge and skills you need to install, configure, build, extend, and deploy a simple events website by using the Jamstack.

Who this book is for

This book is for web developers looking to implement the Jamstack practically. JavaScript developers who want to build modern, speedy, and secure web apps will also find this book useful. Familiarity with JavaScript and database programming is assumed.

What this book covers

Chapter 1, History of the Jamstack, gives you an overview of the history of web design and development and the problems faced with backend-driven websites, namely security, speed, accessibility, hosting, and deployment issues.

Chapter 2, Introduction to Sanity, teaches you how to create a Sanity.io website using the web-based example project creation tool.

Chapter 3, Exploring Sanity Studio, introduces you to Sanity Studio, a structured content management tool. Then, you will learn how to configure the website and create, modify, and delete content.

Chapter 4, Sanity Configuration and Schemas, helps you understand the nomenclature and syntax of Sanity.io's content schemas and how they define the structure of content. You will also learn how to define one-to-one relationships and one-to-many relationships between entities.

Chapter 5, Sanity's GROQ Language, teaches you about GROQ, Sanity.io's proprietary way to query its data. Its similarities and differences with standard SQL will be shown, and various examples will be detailed.

Chapter 6, Sanity's GraphQL Playground, introduces you to Sanity.io's GraphQL playground, how to start it up, and how it differs from standard GraphQL. You will learn how to obtain either a single type of record or multiple.

Chapter 7, Gatsby – An Introduction, teaches you about the *J* part of the Jamstack. You will learn about GatsbyJS, a static generator based on ReactJS, why it was created, how it was built, and the problem it solves. Finally, you will learn about the configuration file and key files involved (such as ssr and node).

Chapter 8, Gatsby and GraphQL, introduces you to Gatsby's GraphQL tool and how it differs from standard GraphQL. This chapter will help you understand how GraphQL is used to connect and serve up, through the Gatsby source code, the sourced content to the static site generator.

Chapter 9, Gatsby Source Plugins, will introduce you to the various plugins that are being built by the Jamstack community that allow GatsbyJS to connect to various types of well-known backend systems, from the filesystem to existing CMS frameworks such as Drupal.

Chapter 10, Building Gatsby Components, will introduce you to the *M* part of the Jamstack, markup, and the building blocks of Gatsby, components, as well as learning how pages, templates, and partials are structured and how they differ. You will learn how to create, edit, and extend components.

Chapter 11, APIs – Extending Gatsby, teaches you about the *A* part of the Jamstack, APIs, and how to use them within the dynamic portion of a compiled web page to recreate the functionality that web developers are familiar with in traditional server-based web development.

Chapter 12, APIs – Alexa Skills, teaches you how to build the Jumpstart Jamstack Alexa skill. As an example, you would be able to ask for the upcoming five events. Through this example, you will be able to extend the current skill by retrieving past events, or all events, and you will also be able to create a new skill for any other application you have.

Chapter 13, Tying It All Together, teaches you how to modify the CSS and the final elements of the website, and how to configure and release a GatsbyJS production build.

Chapter 14, Deployment Using Netlify and Azure, will introduce the Netlify serverless continuous deployment hosting service. You will learn how to connect your websites' repositories to Netlify and how Netlify prepares and combines the various files into a fast, efficiently performing, single static file.

Chapter 15, Conclusion, will summarize the concepts learned throughout the book, discuss how the pieces fit together, and explore how the Jamstack community is evolving. The chapter will discuss various external projects and how to contribute to them.

To get the most out of this book

Software/hardware covered in the book	OS requirements
The React JavaScript framework (Version 16.14.0)	Windows, macOS X, or Linux (any)
The Gatsby frontend framework (Version 2.9.2 or higher)	Windows, macOS X, or Linux (any)
The Sanity.io unified content platform (Version 2.9.1)	Windows, macOS X, or Linux (any)
Netlify (Version 3.18.3)	Windows, macOS X, or Linux (any)
Alexa skills	Windows, macOS X, or Linux (any)

> **Note:**
>
> At the time of writing, latest versions of Gatsby, React, Netlify and Sanity have been used. Any future updates for them will be pushed and updated to the GitHub repository.

If you are using the digital version of this book, we advise you to type the code yourself or access the code via the GitHub repository (link available in the next section). Doing so will help you avoid any potential errors related to copy/pasting of code.

Download the example code files

You can download the example code files for this book from your account at www.packt.com. If you purchased this book elsewhere, you can visit www.packtpub.com/support and register to have the files emailed directly to you.

You can download the code files by following these steps:

1. Log in or register at www.packt.com.
2. Select the **Support** tab.
3. Click on **Code Downloads**.
4. Enter the name of the book in the **Search** box and follow the onscreen instructions.

Once the file is downloaded, please make sure that you unzip or extract the folder using the latest version of:

- WinRAR/7-Zip for Windows
- Zipeg/iZip/UnRarX for Mac
- 7-Zip/PeaZip for Linux

The code bundle for the book is also hosted on GitHub at `https://github.com/PacktPublishing/Jumpstart-Jamstack-Development`. In case there's an update to the code, it will be updated on the existing GitHub repository.

We also have other code bundles from our rich catalog of books and videos available at `https://github.com/PacktPublishing/`. Check them out!

Download the color images

We also provide a PDF file that has color images of the screenshots/diagrams used in this book. You can download it here: `https://static.packt-cdn.com/downloads/9781800203495_ColorImages.pdf`.

Conventions used

There are a number of text conventions used throughout this book.

`Code in text`: Indicates code words in text, database table names, folder names, filenames, file extensions, pathnames, dummy URLs, user input, and Twitter handles. Here is an example: "Mount the downloaded `WebStorm-10*.dmg` disk image file as another disk in your system."

A block of code is set as follows:

```
{
    resolve: "gatsby-source-sanity",
    options: {
        ...clientConfig.sanity,
        token: process.env.SANITY_READ_TOKEN,
        watchMode: !isProd,
        overlayDrafts: !isProd
    }
}
```

When we wish to draw your attention to a particular part of a code block, the relevant lines or items are set in bold:

```
[default]
exten => s,1,Dial(Zap/1|30)
exten => s,2,Voicemail(u100)
exten => s,102,Voicemail(b100)
exten => i,1,Voicemail(s0)
```

Any command-line input or output is written as follows:

```
npm install -g gatsby
```

Bold: Indicates a new term, an important word, or words that you see onscreen. For example, words in menus or dialog boxes appear in the text like this. Here is an example: "Select **System info** from the **Administration** panel."

> **Tips or important notes**
> Appear like this.

Get in touch

Feedback from our readers is always welcome.

General feedback: If you have questions about any aspect of this book, mention the book title in the subject of your message and email us at customercare@packtpub.com.

Errata: Although we have taken every care to ensure the accuracy of our content, mistakes do happen. If you have found a mistake in this book, we would be grateful if you would report this to us. Please visit www.packtpub.com/support/errata, selecting your book, clicking on the Errata Submission Form link, and entering the details.

Piracy: If you come across any illegal copies of our works in any form on the Internet, we would be grateful if you would provide us with the location address or website name. Please contact us at `copyright@packt.com` with a link to the material.

If you are interested in becoming an author: If there is a topic that you have expertise in and you are interested in either writing or contributing to a book, please visit authors. packtpub.com.

Reviews

Please leave a review. Once you have read and used this book, why not leave a review on the site that you purchased it from? Potential readers can then see and use your unbiased opinion to make purchase decisions, we at Packt can understand what you think about our products, and our authors can see your feedback on their book. Thank you!

For more information about Packt, please visit packt.com.

1
History of the Jamstack

Welcome to the **Jamstack**. This completely new web development paradigm has excited the information technology industry and is becoming steadily more popular, with new companies constantly forming around it. This book is one of the first of a few tutorials available focused on practical and hands-on experience with the Jamstack.

A technology *stack* represents a specific collection of languages, databases, and operating systems, such as the LAMP stack. The acronym **LAMP** stands for **Linux**, an operating system; **Apache**, a web server; **MySQL**, a database; and **PHP**, a programming language. The Jamstack is actually not a stack in this sense, but rather a new methodology and toolset to produce websites and web applications.

In this chapter, we're going to first look at the history of the web, introduce the Jamstack, and discuss its advantages. To understand how the Jamstack evolved into what it is today, we need to look back at the more-than-two-decade history of the World Wide Web. Web design and web development, the two main industries that evolved from the World Wide Web, developed into two very popular and lucrative occupations, but it wasn't always that way.

These are the main topics that we will cover in this chapter:

- The evolution of the Jamstack
- The rise of the Jamstack
- Our Jamstack
- Getting started with the Jamstack

The evolution of the Jamstack

The evolution of the Jamstack can be easily explained by looking at how the World Wide Web evolved, starting with its most central component, **HyperText Markup Language (HTML)**.

HTML

The very first web pages were simply comprised of text with HTML tags, providing markup instructions with the ability to link pages together. In fact, HTML is often mistaken by the average person as a programming language, but it was, at the most fundamental level, a series of symbols that represented formatting instructions. It still gets included in programming language lists, together with actual programming languages such as C and Java. It is merely a markup language, though, despite having evolved rapidly to now include accessibility and semantic features. This means that it is not much more than markup. In its earliest versions, however, it simply provided general formatting instructions.

For example, we could use an h1 tag to represent the header of a page, which would make the text appear larger, or a bold tag to make the text bold. Each page would consist of text, links, and HTML tags.

The following code snippet provides an example of this:

```html
<html>
<head>
<title>My Webpage</title>
</head>
<body>
<h1>Welcome to my webpage.</h1>
</body>
<html>
```

As the number of web pages on websites grew, weekly—or even daily—tasks involved updating up to 50 pages manually. Every time a change was needed in a shared part of a web page (such as the header, footer, or navigation pane), these repeated actions proved to be quite tedious.

Let's investigate some solutions that were devised for this problem.

Server-side includes

One attempt to remedy this repeated manual work was called a **server-side include**, or **SSI**. This markup element was created to allow web designers to include pieces of pages (for example, the header) without having to repeat content and markup. Then, when the page was generated, the tag would be replaced with the resultant HTML output.

For example, three links on a web page, Home, About Us, and Contact Us, would have the following markup:

```
<a href="home.html">Home</a>
<a href="about_us.html">About Us</a>
<a href="contact_us.html">Contact Us</a>
```

This HTML could be placed inside a file called navigation.ssi. The include would be called as follows:

```
<!--#include virtual="navigation.ssi" -->
```

After the web server processed this, the result shown on the page would be the same as that shown in the preceding example. Next, another similar approach was used to allow for dynamic content to be produced.

The Common Gateway Interface

The **Common Gateway Interface** or **CGI**, allowed programs written in languages such as Perl to be included in a web page, providing added functionality such as a page counter. The actual place in the HTML page that called this code would again be replaced with the resulting HTML output.

A Perl script that counted the number of page visitors was placed into the cgi-bin directory and called as follows:

```
<p>This page has been visited
<!--#exec cgi="/cgi-bin/counter.pl"--> times.</p>
```

This would produce the following result on the web page:

```
<p>This page has been visited 5349 times.</p>
```

The number 5349 was produced by this code and displayed on the page.

Forms

Another important part of the history of web development was **forms**. Forms allowed a simple web page to transform itself into an actual web application. Web forms replicated the functionality of traditional forms found in desktop applications. Web forms also enabled end users, as opposed to the webmaster, to add content—for example, in forums, submission forms were used.

On the public-facing portion of a website, submissions from these forms added even more content as websites grew quickly in size. Sites soon effectively became software applications, more than just a collection of files with markup. Soon, more than just serving simple pages, web server modules were created to preprocess entire pages as programs.

Web page preprocessors

Another interesting part of the evolution of modern web development was the ability to use whole page preprocessors, such as PHP. In fact, this language, recursively called **PHP: Hypertext Preprocessor**, explains exactly what it does. These files had a different file extension, and the web server (such as Apache) could process the entire page as an actual program and output the result as HTML tags and content.

Next, let's move into the modern era: **Content Management Systems (CMS)**.

Content Management Systems

Soon, databases such as MySQL were included in affordable web hosting plans so that webmasters could easily use them. Database tables could be queried, and the results would enrich and add meaning to many dynamically generated pages. This laid the groundwork for the first CMS.

By allowing website administrators and *webmasters*, as they were historically called, to manage content in databases, *dashboards* or *control panels* were created. A web-based software application entirely separate from the actual website, these administration tools allowed website content to be easily created, edited, and deleted from the website itself.

Again, this caused websites to grow both in size and complexity very rapidly.

WordPress

WordPress quickly rose as the most widely used CMS. Extending the functionality of WordPress, a collection of plugins was developed whereby anybody could develop and install a plugin. This meant that at any one time, a WordPress website could potentially have hundreds of different plugins installed all at the same time.

Most of these were maintained by ambitious volunteers, and new functionality was quickly added. This phenomenon led to rapid release cycles and many different versions of each plugin in use at the same time.

Ajax

Another major innovation was the creation of **Ajax**, or **Asynchronous JavaScript and XML**. Ajax allowed a page to fetch information from a remote source and then, with the result, update that page's content, layout, or style without requiring the page to reload. This *instant update* made websites that still required pages to reload seem cumbersome and slow. Websites again slowly evolved to be one step closer to becoming software applications, similar to desktop applications or single-page applications.

JavaScript frameworks

As the complexity of this dynamic page manipulation grew, **JavaScript frameworks** were born. These helped to reduce development time and enforce best practices. They also provided JavaScript code that could be functional in as many versions of as many browsers as possible. There are still as many as 100 variants of browsers such as Internet Explorer, Firefox, Opera, and Google Chrome running on desktop computers, tablets, and mobile devices.

The rise of the cloud

As the web grew in popularity, web hosting costs decreased. The availability of very low-cost web hosting increased rapidly as many companies entered into the market. Website hosting companies and cloud providers saw an opportunity in this, putting the ability to create a website within reach of almost anybody with very little technical skill, at a very low cost.

As history would show, as with the automobile, sometimes the best inventions also foster many problems. Just as the invention and evolution of the automobile has led to crashes, traffic jams, and safety and security issues—so did websites! Since the majority of websites on the internet were created by amateurs and hosted on servers that were not adequately secured, vulnerabilities on the server were soon discovered and then taken advantage of.

Using a combination of outdated or insecure WordPress plugins, insecure JavaScript, and general misconfiguration of web servers, compromised websites could then be used to send spam emails through utilization of the **Simple Mail Transfer Protocol (SMTP)**. These exploiters inserted email addresses and email contents into database tables and then, in an automated manner, sent thousands of emails per hour, hopefully convincing people to spend money. Keeping a server secure by limiting which tools on the server could be accessed by a user, locking down directories, not allowing repeated login attempts, and other techniques were used to reduce security risk.

However, the overhead of having to make sure that all of a website's plugins were up to date soon became overwhelming. Situations such as version 3.12.26 of a particular plugin not working with version 6.8.14 of another became commonplace. The web slowly became the Wild West!

High-speed access

As high-speed internet became pervasive, connection speeds increased to approach 50-100 **megabits per second (Mbps)** on home computers, through **digital subscriber line (DSL)** and cable internet. Web designers took more liberty regarding the amount of information, images, media files, JavaScript, and anything else that was to be placed on a single web page. This led to a slowing down of what were previously quick-loading websites.

Also, the pages required multiple steps to actually be dynamically generated. Live-running code and database queries needed to be interpreted on each and every request. Page time slowed down because of all of the steps needed to deliver a single web page. As history has shown, a new solution will always arise to address new problems. This solution is called the **Jamstack**.

Let's begin to dissect what it is.

The rise of the Jamstack

The Jamstack represents all that was good about the initial days of web design, together with all of the things that are good about modern web development. Static site generation, as it's sometimes referred to, means simply generating a website comprised of pages that are literally files and nothing more. There is no backend preprocessor and no database, and all of the server complexity is abstracted away.

The Jamstack acronym explained

The Jamstack acronym stands for **JavaScript, APIs, and Markup**. Since a static site page cannot be produced by any real-time preprocessing, all dynamic aspects of the page must be achieved through JavaScript, which will perform all page interactions.

JavaScript will communicate with external systems, such as search engines, using **application programming interfaces** (**APIs**). The use of APIs is a modern way of either leveraging pre-built external **Software-as-a-Service** (**SAAS**), such as Algolia's search API, or using another software application that would previously exist on the same server as the static site. Limiting communication to APIs allows each component of a larger system to remain independent and reusable.

Finally, Markup represents the page itself. As mentioned, HTML is a language that it used to create web pages. Sometimes, Markdown is incorrectly used in the place of Markup. Markdown is actually one of the notations used to produce markup; however, there are many different ways to produce markup.

Jamstack advantages

Now, let's learn about the advantages of the Jamstack.

Speed

As mentioned before, one of the advantages of static pages is that each page is actually a file on the filesystem. As in the early days of web design, each file is loaded through a web server. The only bottleneck is the speed of accessing the file, reading it, and then sending its contents through the web server.

A **Content Delivery Network** (**CDN**) is a network of many servers placed all over the world. This means that the pages will be optimally served from the nearest server to the website user, reducing network latency. This represents an overall faster and better experience for the end user.

All of the **Cascading Style Sheets** (**CSS**) and JavaScript will usually be minified or compressed in a way that removes unnecessary characters, spaces, tabs, line breaks, and other non-essential items. The fewest number of characters are used and combined together in one or more files as a way of reducing the number of files involved.

Non-minified JavaScript looks like this:

```
<javascript>
function multiplyTwoNumbers(number1, number2){
    return number1 * number2;
```

```
    }
var result = multiplyTwoNumbers(2,3);
</javascript>
```

Minified JavaScript looks like this:

```
<javascript>
function a(b,c){return b*c;}var d=a(2,3);
</javascript>
```

Less error-prone

Most Jamstack systems have a build process that checks all of the HTML, JavaScript, and CSS for correctness during the process that builds the pages, so a serious coding error will cause the build to fail, not allowing the error to actually make it into production.

Security

Using the safe **HyperText Transfer Protocol Secure** (**HTTPS**) instead of the older **HyperText Transfer Protocol** (**HTTP**) means that all information transmitted will be secure, as it is encrypted from end to end.

Also, since static pages are served through *serverless* hosting services, there is no chance that any backend systems or databases could be compromised. No longer is there a need to spend valuable time keeping the server, libraries, login access, and mail services secure and always on the latest version, or even worrying about conflicts between the various versions.

Developer experience

Developing in the Jamstack means using popular and modern programming languages, such as JavaScript, TypeScript, and **ECMAScript 6** (**ES6**) variants. Jamstack developers may also take advantage of modern query languages such as GraphQL, and libraries and frameworks such as ReactJS and VueJS. They may also use static site generators such as Hugo and GatsbyJS.

Our Jamstack

As should be clear by now, the Jamstack is not a stack, but rather a web development paradigm. Any combination of the various components of the Jamstack ecosystem may be used. For this book, we will use three of the most popular software applications and services to produce a Jamstack website: GatsbyJS, Sanity.io, and Netlify. We will also provide several examples, using other Jamstack tools for comparison.

GatsbyJS

One of the most popular parts of the Jamstack that is actually a static site generator is GatsbyJS.

GatsbyJS (referred to as Gatsby) is open source and uses the React JavaScript library to compile and build static pages from various sources. These sources may be as simple as a filesystem; a collection of Markdown files; a traditional CMS such as WordPress or Drupal; or a headless CMS such as Contentful or Sanity.

Sanity.io

Since the *Jamstack way* of doing web development eschews a single, monolithic CMS, the actual content that a website needs is separate from the tools that will format it and deliver it.

Sanity.io (referred to as Sanity) is a platform for structured content. There is an open source CMS called Sanity Studio, which enables content producers such as writers, editors, and photographers to easily create rich content that is flexible and modular, without the need to understand programming and markup languages.

Netlify

The actual *hosting* of the website will be done on a serverless system.

Netlify is a service that enables a developer to enjoy fully automated compilation and deployment onto Netlify's CDN, pushing content out quickly and safely to servers throughout the world.

Getting started with the Jamstack

Now that we have learned about the history of the Jamstack and its advantages, we will next look at the tools necessary to use the Jamstack in the context of this book.

Installation

Installing all of the pieces of a Jamstack development environment and configuring everything to work properly will be daunting for developers who are new to the technology, so the best approach is to refer to each of the components' websites for up-to-date installation and configuration documentation.

This book has an accompanying GitHub repository with all of the code necessary to perform all of the examples. Therefore, the first tool that needs to be installed will be the Git version control system. Users who are new to Git will find a vast amount of information, cheat sheets, and help forums for its usage, but most of the basic operations are performed with only four or five commands. Many code editors, such as WebStorm, have the commands built into the user interface.

To ensure that the installation process is up to date, the README.md file in the provided repository will provide installation instructions and links to each project's current documentation.

Prerequisites

Several web development tools are necessary to work with the examples in this book, and these are listed here:

- Terminal
- Node.js and **node package manager** (npm)
- Git
- An **Integrated Development Environment** (**IDE**) or text editor

A Terminal environment will be needed to execute commands. Which Terminal application should be used will vary depending on the operating system used.

Node.js allows JavaScript to be run in the Terminal, not only in the browser.

npm is necessary for the installation of both Sanity and Gatsby. This allows many packages that are groups of JavaScript functionality to be installed.

The Git command-line version control system is essential for the installation of Gatsby and also to download the examples in this book.

Finally, an IDE that provides code syntax highlighting and linting, which continually analyzes the code for correctness, is needed. If this is not possible, a text editor is needed to modify the source code files. As of this writing, Visual Studio Code and WebStorm are two popular IDE choices.

Optional tools

Optionally, Yarn may be used for the examples in this book. Yarn is an npm-compatible replacement for npm and while it is suggested, it is not required.

Summary

In this chapter, we learned about how the World Wide Web grew from simple pages with markup and links, to become massively slow and insecure web applications. We learned how the Jamstack combines various aspects of the past and present to form a truly modern, decoupled, and enjoyable paradigm to work with for web developers and web designers wishing to learn more.

In the next chapter, we'll begin our journey into the construction of a real, working Jamstack application. We'll become familiar with Sanity and a web-based tool to quickly create a sample application, using one of several templates.

We will introduce Sanity and its features and show how to modify its schemas. We will show how to use Sanity to design and build the structured content needed to create a website with news and events.

2
Introduction to Sanity

Throughout this book, we will build a news and events website and make use of Sanity.io as a structured content framework. We will explore how to create and manage content and new types of content by adding custom fields, defining validation rules for the fields, and customizing Sanity Studio. We will also learn how to *source* our content to a frontend framework through the **Graph-Relational Object Queries (GROQ)** Sanity.io query language and GraphQL.

We will make use of JavaScript React-based Gatsby as our frontend framework and we will run through the components of the framework, showing how to manage routes, pages, and single components such as images, calendars, forms, listings, and more.

We will host the application on Netlify, which is a platform for automating the deployment of web projects. We will manage our code through the GitHub distributed source code versioning system and connect it to Netlify, in order to trigger automated deployment every time we add a new feature to our code repository.

This chapter will cover the following main topics:

- Account setup
- Introduction to Sanity.io
- Creating a project

- Introducing Sanity Manage
- Sanity Studio overview

Technical requirements

You will require the following things to understand this chapter:

- A GitHub account
- A Sanity Studio account
- A Netlify account

The code for this chapter can be found at `https://github.com/PacktPublishing/Jumpstart-Jamstack-Development/tree/chapter_two`.

Account setup

The first step required is to create an account on the Sanity.io website (`https://www.sanity.io`). A Sanity account may be set up at the start of the project creation. The three different methods for creating an account are with a Google account, a GitHub account, or simply with an email and password. Next, we create an account on the Netlify website (`https://app.netlify.com/signup`). There are four methods that may be used for account creation: GitHub, GitLab, a Bitbucket account, or email and password. We will be using GitHub as it is the most convenient option. Finally, if not already created, create an account on the GitHub website (`https://github.com/join`). A username, email address, and password are required.

At the time of writing, all three services use the freemium model and thus provide a generous free plan for use with small projects.

Introduction to Sanity.io

"Sanity.io is the platform for structured content."

– `https://www.sanity.io/docs`

Sanity.io is a data storage service where you can manage content, making use of Sanity's **Application Programming Interfaces (APIs)**, tools, and libraries. You can easily build a centralized content repository for your projects.

Sanity at its core is the data store and its query language is GROQ.

Since Sanity Studio is an open source single-page application, it can be freely modified and themed. Built using the JavaScript language, you can easily define your content structure. Then, using the ReactJS library, you are able to extend Sanity Studio's functionality with your own ReactJS components. Also, Sanity Studio enables workflow personalization for a project's content editors. Since Sanity Studio uses npm, you may contribute a plugin by creating a public package hosted on `https://www.npmjs.com/`, to extend its functionality.

Sanity's content is stored and accessed via its data store, which is accessible using either the Sanity.io client library or via a **HyperText Transfer Protocol (HTTP)** API call. Sanity.io manages the data store, which is cloud-hosted.

What is GROQ?

GROQ is a query language created by Sanity. It is used to retrieve information from the data store. GROQ is easy to learn and powerful—for example, different sets of documents can be queried into a single response.

Now that we have a high-level overview of Sanity.io, we will create our first project.

Creating a project

After you have successfully created accounts on Sanity.io, GitHub, and Netlify, we can begin with the project creation, using the Sanity.io **Blog with Gatsby** starter project.

The **Uniform Resource Locator (URL)** for Sanity.io project creation is `https://www.sanity.io/create`.

Click on the **Create project** link, as shown in the following screenshot:

Figure 2.1 – Sanity create page

There are three steps to complete for creating our very first project, as follows:

1. Log in to your Sanity.io account using one of the aforementioned methods, and add the **Project title**. Sanity needs this section to create a new Sanity project for you. We can set the **Project title** as <Your Name> hands-on Jamstack. The following screenshot shows an example of this:

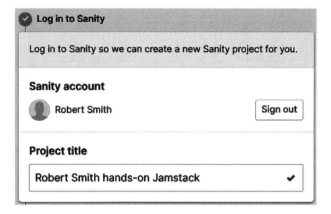

Figure 2.2 – Connect to Sanity.io

Sanity will create a repository for the project. Click the **Sign In** button to connect to your GitHub account and rename the repository as *your-name-hands-on-Jamstack*.

> **Note**
>
> You cannot have any spaces in the name.

Optionally, you may set it as a private repository. On each git push to the remote repository, the website will be automatically redeployed, as illustrated in the following screenshot:

Figure 2.3 – Connect to GitHub

Sanity will automatically deploy your application to Netlify and make it available to the web.

2. Click the **Connect** button to connect to your Netlify account, and we are ready to go! You should see the following message:

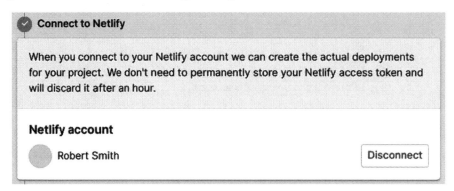

Figure 2.4 – Connect to Netlify

3. Now, press the **Create project** button, as illustrated in the following screenshot, and in a short amount of time the project will be set up:

Figure 2.5 – Create project

Once the project is created, Sanity will deploy two web applications to Netlify.

The first web application is the frontend website driven by Gatsby that connects to the Sanity-hosted backend.

The URL structure format is as follows:

```
https://website-name.netlify.com
```

You can see that it takes the form of the project name plus the Netlify domain.

The other web application is Sanity Studio, where we can manage the content. The URL structure format is as follows:

```
https://website-name-studio.netlify.com
```

You can see that it takes the form of project name, a dash, the word `studio`, and then the Netlify domain.

Let's start exploring Sanity.

Introducing Sanity Manage

Let's start by looking at the Sanity.io project we have just created. Log in to your Sanity.io account by clicking on the **Log in** link on the Sanity.io website, as shown in the following screenshot:

Log in

Figure 2.6 – Log in link

After logging in, you should be able to see a list of your projects. From the top menu, you will also have the option to create a new team and the option to create a new project as illustrated in the following screenshot:

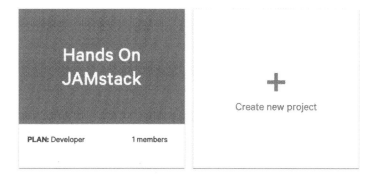

Figure 2.7 – Sanity.io Manage landing page

Click on the project's rectangular block, and let's have a look at the project pages.

Sanity.io project pages

From this section, you can manage your Sanity.io project. Under the top menu, you can find the section with project's Sanity Studio details such as URL, **PROJECT ID**, and **PLAN** will always be visible across all the pages of the project as illustrated in the following screenshot:

Figure 2.8 – Sanity menu header

Under this top menu, there is a second-level menu with various aspects of the project, as illustrated in the following screenshot:

Figure 2.9 – Second-level menu

There are five sections to be explored. Let's take a look at each one in turn.

Usage

In this section of the page, the resource usage presented as bandwidth in **kilobytes (KB)**, **megabytes (MB)**, or **gigabytes (GB)** for this project is shown.

There are currently seven charts available, with the following data:

- **Resource Usage**:

  Document used (a donut chart)

  Assets used (a donut chart)

- **Usage this month**:

  Bandwidth (an area graph)

  API Requests (an area graph)

  API CDN Requests (an area graph)

- **Asset and document history**:

  Documents (an area graph)

  Assets (an area graph)

Bandwidth, document, and request statistics are updated once every hour. Asset statistics are updated once a day.

Members

On the **Members** page, all members of the current project are displayed. Here, users may invite and remove members, depending on their role. When adding a new member, they may choose the type of access level for this member.

There are three permissions that can be set, as follows:

- **Administrator**: A user with this role can fully manage the current project and its aspects.

- **Read + Write**: A user with this role can read from and write to all datasets of the current project.

- **Read**: A user with this role can only read from all datasets of the current project.

Datasets

From this section, you may view and remove datasets. Datasets are where data is stored. A project may have more than one dataset, depending on the project's needs. The *Developer* account is limited to two accounts.

Settings

From this section, you can manage the **General settings** and **API** of the current project.

General settings include the following:

- **Organization**
- **Project Name**
- **Project Color**
- **Custom Studio URL**

You can also disable or delete a project. When you disable a project, it can be re-enabled at any time without data loss.

When you delete a project, all the documents, assets, and users related to the project will be removed. **Note that this action cannot be undone**.

From this section, you may also view and modify your current plan. Depending on your needs, you can choose a different plan. For this project, though, the free plan Developer is amply sufficient, providing up to three users.

Let's explore the **API** settings, in the following subsections.

CORS Origins

In this subsection, you can add and remove hosts that can connect to the project API. The `localhost:3333` host is automatically added. `localhost:3333` is our local development environment URL. The Gatsby application URL and Sanity Studio application URL hosted on Netlify are also automatically added to the **CORS Origins** list.

In this way, we allow our local development environment and the applications hosted on Netlify to access our Sanity API.

Every time we want to let a new application communicate with the Sanity API, we do this by simply adding the application URL to our **CORS Origins** list, which is as follows:

- **Token**: A token is used by robots to query the project API.
- **Webhooks**: Webhooks are called when an action is triggered. For example, when content is changed, we can call a given URL to perform an action such as a notification.

Now that we know how to change the configuration of our application, let's see how we can add content through Sanity Studio.

Sanity Studio overview

The starter project is a blog site where a user may add the following:

- Blog posts
- Authors
- Categories

Throughout this book, we are going to extend this functionality by creating a news and events website, adding new types of content and new types of fields.

We will manage the application settings and content from Sanity Studio.

Click on the **Studio** link from the Sanity Studio details section given below the top-level menu.

The first screen contains the Sanity Studio **Dashboard**, where there are some useful widgets that we are going to explore now.

Navigation

From the **Navigation** menu, all sections of Sanity Studio may be accessed, as illustrated in the following screenshot:

Figure 2.10 – Sanity Studio navigation menu

Clicking on the Pencil sign will open a pop-up where you can choose to add a **Blog post**, an **Author**, or a **Category**.

From the **Search** field, you can look for any **Blog post**, **Author**, and **Category**.

Dashboard and **Desk** are the two main sections of the application. Let's discuss these in detail.

Dashboard

In the **Dashboard** section, we have shortcuts divided in blocks that link to all the sections included in Sanity Studio.

Edit your content

From this shortcut, the user has access to subpages of the **Desk** section, such as the following:

- **Settings**
- **Blog posts**
- **Authors**
- **Categories**

Netlify sites

This block lists the Netlify sites created for a project. We can click **View** or **Admin** to perform operations on our application. If any website content is changed, a deployment may be triggered by clicking on the **Deploy** button.

Sanity Studio is the application we are currently using, and **Blog Website** is our blog application.

Project info

This block lists all information relating to Sanity projects, as follows:

- Project ID
- Dataset
- Frontend
- GROQ
- GraphQL
- GitHub repository

Project users

Similar to the **Team** section of the **Sanity Manage** page, **Project users** lists all the current project's users.

Recent blog posts

As the block title indicates, a list of five recent blog posts will be shown here. Clicking on each blog post title will bring you to the **Edit** page for that specific blog post.

Desk

From the **Desk** section of Sanity Studio, the settings and content may be managed.

Settings

The application comes with some basic settings that we will extend during this book.

Basic settings include the following:

- **Title**
- **Description**
- **Keywords**
- **Author**

Blog posts

A **blog post** is a piece of content created by an author. It comes with some preconfigured fields, such as the following:

- **Title**
- **Slug**
- **Published at**
- **Main image**
- **Excerpt**
- **Authors**
- **Categories**
- **Body**

Authors

Authors are the creators of a piece of content, such as a blog post. Similar to **Blog post**, this section has preconfigured fields, such as the following:

- **Name**
- **Slug**
- **Image**
- **Biography**

Categories

Categories are used to categorize a piece of content. A category may be also used to filter content during a search.

As with the **Blog posts** and **Authors** sections, it has a few predefined fields, namely **Title** and **Description**.

Summary

In this chapter, we were introduced to Sanity.io. Through Sanity's **Create** tool we have created a new application hosted on Netlify using the Sanity user interface, and we have hosted our code base on GitHub. We explored how to manage a Sanity application and Sanity Studio's **Dashboard** capabilities.

In the next chapter, we will explore the example content, and learn how to delete, modify, and create new content using the Sanity Studio **Desk**.

3
Exploring Sanity Studio

Now that we have a basic Jamstack application installed and configured and have learned about the basic sections of the dashboard and desk, we will begin to build a news and events website based on the example blog that is created.

The main topics that we will cover in this chapter are as follows:

- Modifying the example author
- Removing and adding articles
- Modifying the website settings and redeploying the website

In the Sanity Studio dashboard, the **Recent blog posts** widget will display a few example articles, so the first step will be to remove those articles and add our own.

Technical requirements

A web browser is needed.

Modifying the example author

The sample author created in the previous chapter is simply an example, so we will modify and personalize the author to our own name. Follow along with each step as we use Sanity Studio to modify the author.

Modifying the existing author

Follow these steps in order to learn how to do this task:

1. Click the **Desk** icon in the top navigation bar, as shown:

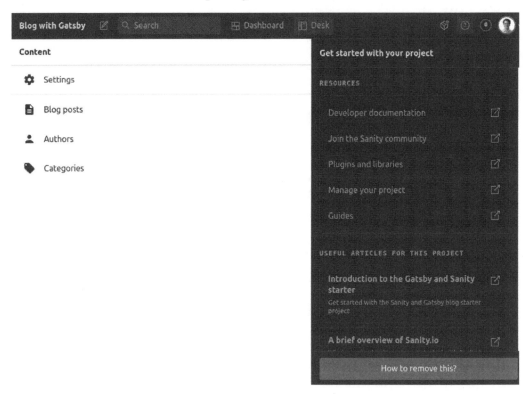

Figure 3.1 – Sanity Studio

While **Dashboard** provides a broad overview of the contents, **Desk** provides a means to view, create, modify, and delete the project's contents.

2. Click **Authors** in the **Content** navigation menu (located on the left), as shown:

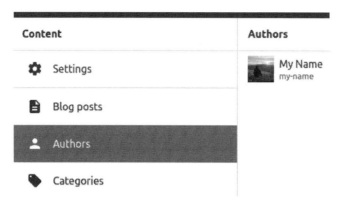

Figure 3.2 – Authors navigation menu item

3. Click on the example author, **My Name**, in this case.

4. Change **Name** to your actual name. Here, the name **Christopher John Pecoraro** is used as an example.

5. Click the **Generate** button to generate a new slug. This will be the URL used for the author's profile page.

6. Click the **Upload** button to upload a new image.

7. Modify the caption and alternative text as appropriate.

8. Modify the biography as appropriate.

   At this point, the article should be showing a draft status. This author is not saved yet:

Figure 3.3 – Draft status

9. Click the **Publish** button:

Figure 3.4 – Publish button

At this point, the author profile is published and should be displaying a **Published** status. The latest version of it will be available for use:

Figure 3.5 – Published notification

Notice that the **Content** menu is collapsed like an accordion, as shown in the following screenshot. The text is displayed vertically:

Figure 3.6 – Author entry

Clicking on the **Content** bar will display the topmost menu again in **Desk**.

Creating an additional author

At this point, we only have one author; however, most news websites have more than one author, so follow these steps to create a second author:

1. Click **Authors** in the **Content** navigation menu (located on the left), as shown:

Figure 3.7 – Authors menu item

2. Click on the pencil icon to create an additional author, as shown:

Figure 3.8 – Authors header and add new icon

3. Enter a first and last name.

4. Click the **Generate** button to generate a new slug.

5. Optionally, upload an avatar or profile picture.

6. Add a caption and alternative text.

7. Enter a biography.

8. Click the **Publish** button as in the previous section:

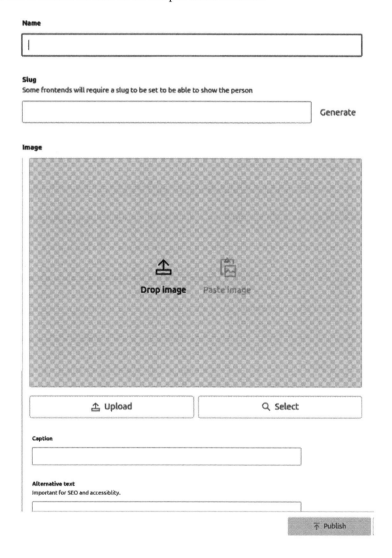

Figure 3.9 – New author details

We have replaced the example author with two new authors. Similarly, there is additional example content that needs to be dealt with. In the same way that in this section an example author was created, several example articles were created, too.

Removing and adding articles

Now we will remove these articles and begin to create our own content. This will allow us to create our own website.

Removing example articles

Follow these steps to remove the example articles:

1. Click on **Blog posts** in the main **Content** menu. Click on the first article.

2. At the bottom of the interface, there is a context menu on the right side of the floating bar, next to the **Publish** button. Click the down arrow icon and a menu will appear as shown. **Delete** will be one of the options; click it:

Figure 3.10 – Publish menu

3. A confirmation dialog menu will appear, so click the **Delete now** button:

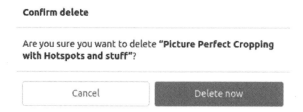

Figure 3.11 – Delete confirmation modal

4. Repeat *steps 1–3* for each of the articles.

Now that we have removed all of the articles, we will add our first news article.

Creating a new article

Follow the steps to create a new article:

1. From the main **Content** menu, click the **Blog posts** menu item.

2. Click on the pencil icon to create a new article.

3. Enter a title for the article.

4. Click **Generate** to generate the slug.

5. Select a **Published at** date. At the time of writing, this must be selected and not left as is with the placeholder text:

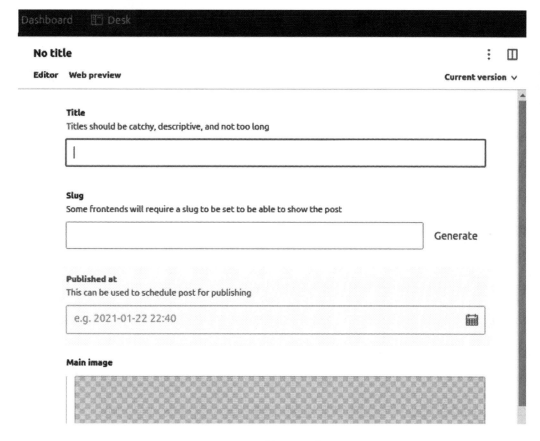

Figure 3.12 – New blog post form, part 1

6. Upload an image by clicking the **Upload** button.

7. Enter a **Caption** and **Alternative text**:

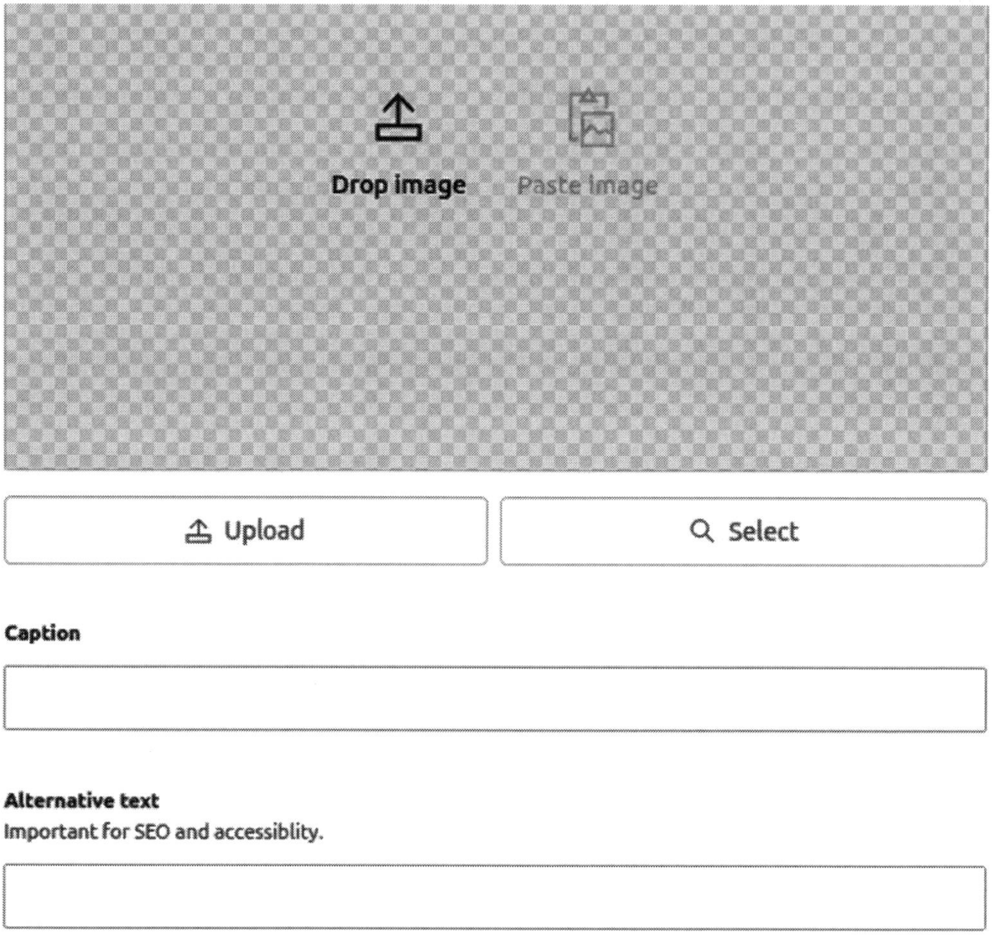

Figure 3.13 – New blog post form, part 2

8. Complete the **Excerpt** section by writing a short summary of the article.

9. Select the author by clicking on the **Add** button and selecting a name and then clicking the **Close** button.

10. Optionally, select a category.

11. Complete the **Body** section by entering the contents of the article:

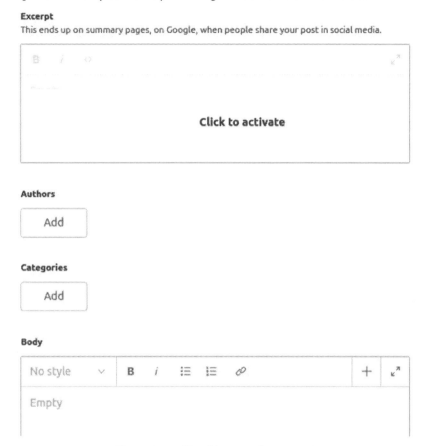

Figure 3.14 – New blog post form, part 3

12. Click the **Publish** button as in the previous example to publish. The status should change from **DRAFT** (as indicated by a pencil icon next to the title in the **Blog posts** menu) to **Published**.

Modifying the website settings and redeploying the website

Lastly, we need to modify the website settings. After everything is set up correctly, the next step will be to redeploy the website with the changes that we have performed in this chapter.

Setting the website name

Returning to the main **Content** menu, click the **Settings** menu item. These settings are the title of the website, a description, a list of keywords, and the website author. For this example, the title will be News and Events:

1. Modify the title.

2. Modify the description.

3. Click the **Publish** button on the bottom bar:

Figure 3.15 – Settings form

At this point, we have learned about Sanity Studio's basic functionality through creating, deleting, and modifying content using Sanity Studio. Next, we will instruct Netlify to deploy a new version of the website. Netlify will run scripts to enable Gatsby to use the new content together with its templates to create a new version.

Redeployment through Netlify

Follow these steps to redeploy the website using the Netlify platform:

1. Click on the **Dashboard** icon to return to the dashboard, as shown in the following screenshot:

Figure 3.16 – Link to the dashboard

2. Click the **Deploy** button that corresponds to the blog website, as shown:

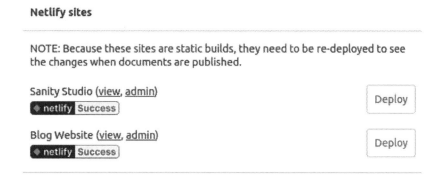

Figure 3.17 – Netlify sites list

The status will change from **Success** (green-colored) to **Building** (orange-colored) during the build process, as shown in the following screenshot:

Figure 3.18 – Netlify Building status

The build time will vary, but eventually, the status will return to **Success**.

3. Click the website URL that corresponds to **Frontend** to view the changes. A reload of the page may be required:

Figure 3.19 – Project info section

4. The website will display an article with its excerpt, as shown in *Figure 3.20*:

Figure 3.20 – Article excerpt

Summary

In this chapter, we have learned how to use the basic features of Sanity Studio. We are now able to configure basic website information based on the initial example content. We can add, modify, and delete the various content elements. We cannot yet modify the structure of Sanity's documents, though.

In the next chapter, we will learn about Sanity's entities and their relations.

4

Sanity Configuration and Schemas

In the previous chapter, we learned how to use Sanity Studio. In this chapter, we will learn how to clone the project from GitHub, install its dependencies, learn how to start up the local development environment, and examine the file structure. Then, we will learn how schemas are constructed, and how to modify them, learning about relationships. This will allow you to easily make modifications to the schema, testing the schema locally by viewing it in the hosted version in the browser.

The main topics that we will cover in this chapter are the following:

- Modeling content with schemas
- Schema relationships
- Extending, modifying, and deploying the schema

Technical requirements

A Terminal or Terminal emulator.

The code files for this chapter are placed at `https://github.com/PacktPublishing/Jumpstart-Jamstack-Development/tree/chapter_four`.

Modeling content with schemas

The schema is the heart of Sanity. It is a file that defines the structure of an entity, which could either represent something physical that occurs in nature, for example, a person, such as an author, or something abstract, such as a category, as demonstrated in *Chapter 3, Exploring Sanity Studio*. These structures and the collections of them, optionally linked together, are what drives the user experience in Sanity Studio.

In the next sections, we will clone the project, and work with the project's schemas.

Cloning the project

In *Chapter 3, Exploring Sanity Studio*, the `create` tool automatically created a repository in GitHub. To clone a repository, the `git` command-line tool is needed. Git is a source code management tool created by the inventor of the Linux kernel, Linus Torvalds. Installation instructions for each operating system can be found at `https://git-scm.com/`.

Following the standard steps for cloning a repository, type the following command in the Terminal:

```
git clone repository-name
```

The `repository-name` should be replaced with the actual name of your repository. To clone the repository, which creates a local copy, locate the repository that was automatically created in GitHub.

The repository may be cloned using one of two methods:

- The first method uses SSH, where the username is the GitHub `username` and `repository` is the actual repository:

  ```
  git clone git@github.com:username/repository.git
  ```

This is shown in the following screenshot:

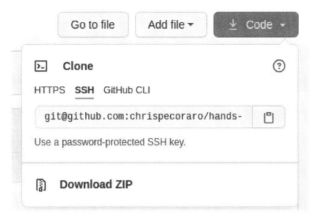

Figure 4.1 – The GitHub Code clone modal – SSH mode

- The second method uses HTTPS, where `username` is the GitHub username and `repository` is the actual repository. Note the slightly different format than the SSH method:

```
git clone https://github.com/username/repository.git
```

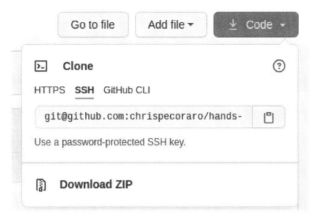

Figure 4.2 – The GitHub Code clone modal – HTTPS mode

Both these methods will create a folder at the same filesystem level with the name of the repository. The SSH method allows a password-protected SSH key to be used, so it is the preferred method.

Exploring the project's folders

In this section, we shall examine the contents of the project's folders and files. There are several important files as well as several folders. The first file that we will examine is the sanity.json file. This file is located in the project's studio folder.

Examining the sanity.json file

Here are the first few lines of the sanity.json file:

```
{
  "root": true,
  "project": {
    "name": "Hands On JAMstack"
  },
  "api": {
    "projectId": "abc123d4",
    "dataset": "production"
  },
```

This file contains two important values: projectId and the dataset name:

- projectId: The projectId value uniquely defines the project, meaning that no one else will have this ID. The projectId consists of letters and numbers.

- dataset: The dataset value, however, is not unique, and will be used to identify which dataset this instance of Sanity Studio is currently using. For example, one might select production to represent a final version of a schema and data, and development to represent the upcoming changes. Both the schema and the actual content are contained within the dataset. Each dataset is completely separate, and Sanity Studio may load any one of the datasets, but only one schema at a time.

Additionally, the root is set to true to specify that this file is the project's main sanity.json file, since plugins may have their own sanity.json files. The sanity.json files found in plugins will have root set to true.

Examining the schemas folder

Next, we shall examine the `schemas` folder in the `studio` folder. In the two subfolders – `documents` and `objects`, we will find a collection of files, one per schema. Each one is a JavaScript file with a single object. The following code example shows a schema file format with minimal fields:

```
export default {
    name: 'siteSettings',
    type: 'document',
    title: 'Site Settings',
}
```

The file begins with the `export` keyword. The `export` keyword means that this JavaScript module may be used in the calling file by using the `import` statement. The next keyword is `default`. This keyword means that this single object will be used. Finally, the object itself follows, using the opened and closed parentheses.

The three essential attributes in the object, which are key and value attribute pairs, are `name`, `title`, and `type`.

name

The `name` attribute used in schemas always represents a single entity. The `name` value must be a single word, and per convention should match the name of the file, but without the extension, of course.

Camel case, named as such because of the animal that it most looks like, is used. The standard format is as follows: the first word is represented as lowercase, and the second word and words that follow are capitalized. For example, a correct name attribute value would be `siteSettings`.

title

The next important attribute is `title`. This attribute is meant to be a human-readable description of the schema entity and may contain spaces and other special characters. It is displayed inside Sanity Studio. Therefore, it should be a word that clearly defines what it represents. For example, the corresponding title could be `Site Settings`.

type

Next, the schema type determines whether the schema is a document or object. A document is what will be listed in the main navigation of Sanity Studio. An object is a more abstract representation of an entity, such as a relationship between two documents or a building block to be used within a document, such as an address block containing several fields, such as address, city, and postal code.

The default project that is automatically created uses the two directories – documents and objects, to help organize the project by grouping the schemas by type.

Author schema

For the next step, examine the structure of the author.js file in the documents directory.

Schema definition

As shown in the following code sample, the fields attribute is an array. The use of square brackets is a syntax to denote a list or collection of items. To begin with, the list of items is empty. It will be filled to contain a list of fields:

```
export default {
    name: 'author',
    type: 'document',
    title: 'Author',
    fields: [
        ],
}
```

All entities must contain at least one field. Each object within the fields array follows the same format as the entity itself, at a minimum name, title, and type.

Schema fields

Possibly the simplest example of this would be a name field, which represents the first and last name of the author:

```
export default {
    name: 'author',
    type: 'document',
    title: 'Author',
```

```
    fields: [
        {
            name: 'name',
            type: 'string',
            title: 'Name'
        },
    ],
}
```

In the preceding code example, we have placed the `name` attributes inside of the `fields` array. This array is of a string type, which basically means a short phrase or label without any associated formatting such as bold italics.

> **Note**
>
> The `title` attribute should represent a word or phrase that a content editor could recognize and will be displayed in Sanity Studio.

There are three other attributes that can be used in each field:

- `description` is a longer description of how the field should be used.
- `readOnly` disables editing in Sanity Studio.
- `hidden` hides the field from Sanity Studio.

The `readOnly` and `hidden` fields would be modified programmatically and not by the person using the interface.

Schema field types

There is a wide range of types available for use. At the time of writing, the following types, other than `document`, are available:

- Array
- Block
- Boolean
- Date
- Datetime
- File
- Geopoint

- Image
- Number
- Object
- Reference
- Slug
- String
- Span
- Text
- URL

Some of these types are primitives. A **primitive** is a very simple piece of information, such as a Boolean value, which would be only one of two values, either `true` or `false`. Additionally, a number type is simply a numeric value. Other types, such as `image`, are more complex and contain multiple fields.

> **Note**
>
> The complete documentation on the current types available for Sanity schemas may be found at `https://www.sanity.io/docs/schema-types`.

We have learned about how schemas are constructed, so now let's look at how these schemas could be connected through relationships.

Schema relationships

Relationships between documents are called **references**. These references allow a schema to be used in another in various ways, so let's examine the various ways.

A one-to-one relationship

A reference connects one document to another. This is called a **one-to-one** relationship. An example of a one-to-one relationship might be a person and their street address.

The street address might only belong to one person. The address entity might have the following structure:

```
export default {
  name: 'address',
```

```
  type: 'document',
  title: 'Address',
  fields: [
{
  name: 'street',
  type: 'string',
  title: 'Street'
},
{
  name: 'city',
  type: 'string',
  title: 'City'
},
{
  name: 'postalCode',
  type: 'string',
  title: 'Postal Code'
},
{
  name: 'country',
  type: 'string',
  title: 'Country'
},
  ],
}
```

In this example, this schema is of type address, so author will link to address through the address reference as shown:

```
export default {
  name: 'author',
  type: 'document',
  title: 'Author',
  fields: [
  {
    name: 'name',
    type: 'string',
```

```
        title: 'Name'
    },
    {
      name: 'address'
      type: 'reference'
      to: {type: 'address'}
    }
    ],
}
```

In the Sanity schema, we use the reference type and an additional attribute, `to`. The `to` attribute accepts an object specifying the type.

A one-to-many relationship

In the same way, a schema can be related to many schemas, even of various types. A simple example is an author that writes for multiple publishing houses:

```
{
  name: 'publishers',
  title: 'Publishers',
  type: 'array',
  of: [
    {
      type: 'reference',
      to: '[{type: 'publisher'}],
    }
  ]
},
```

In this example, the `type` field is an array so that inside Sanity Studio, one or more publishers could be chosen from a list of publishers. Note that the name `"publishers"` is given to this field to show that this field represents multiple publishers, however, the relationship is to a schema of type `publisher`, and schema names are always singular.

In the first part of this chapter, we learned about the structure of a schema. In the next section, we will learn how to modify schemas.

Extending, modifying, and deploying the schema

For the example used in this book, we will be creating a news and events website. The first step in this process is to create a file named event.js in the document directory, which will represent our event schema.

The event schema

The following code segment is the schema for an event, illustrating its various fields:

```
export default {
  name: 'event',
  type: 'document',
  title: 'Event',
  fields: [
    {
      name: 'name',
      type: 'string',
      title: 'Name'
    },
    {
      name: 'dateAndTime',
      type: 'datetime',
      title: 'Date and Time'
    },
    {
      name: 'venue',
      type: 'reference',
      to: {type: 'venue'}
    },
    {
      name: 'virtual',
      type: 'boolean',
      title: 'Virtual Event'
    },
    {
      name: 'eventUrl',
```

```
      type: 'url',
      title: 'URL'
    },
    {
      name: 'body',
      type: 'bodyPortableText',
      title: 'Body'
    }
  ]
}
```

At this point, most of the file should appear familiar. The event date and time will use a special `datetime` field type that will present a nice calendar to the user. The event will be linked to a venue if it is not a virtual event. Whether or not the event is virtual, it will be represented by a Boolean value.

Lastly, `bodyPortableText` is a special field type; it is actually its own schema, representing a more advanced structure, as well as instructions on how it will be used.

The venue schema

The next step is to create a file named `venue.js` in the `documents` directory. This file will, as expected, represent a venue:

```
export default {
  name: 'venue',
  type: 'document',
  title: 'Venue',
  fields: [
    {
      name: 'name',
      type: 'string',
      title: 'Name'
    },
    {
      name: 'description',
      type: 'bodyPortableText',
      title: 'Description'
    },
```

```
        {
          name: 'location',
          type: 'geopoint',
          title: 'Location'
        },
        {
          name: 'telephone',
          type: 'string',
          title: 'Telephone'
        },
        {
          name: 'email',
          type: 'string',
          title: 'Email'
        },
        {
          name: 'website',
          type: 'url',
          title: 'Website'
        },
    ]
}
```

The venue schema also contains some useful field types, such as geopoint, which will allow us to take advantage of the Google Maps API to automatically complete an address, and a URL that provides input validation.

The schemas folder should now have the following files:

```
schemas
  documents
    author.js
    category.js
    event.js
    post.js
    siteSettings.js
    venue.js
```

The schema file

For Sanity to be able to recognize a new schema, that schema must be added to the
schema.js file, which is in the studio/schemas folder. Let's see how to do so:

1. Add the files via import statements at the top of the file, after the line starting with
    import siteSettings:

```
// document schemas
import siteSettings from './documents/siteSettings'
//insert these two rows
import event from './documents/event'
import venue from './documents/venue'
```

2. Add the imported schema to the list of schema types:

```
types: schemaTypes.concat([
    // The following are document types which will appear
    // in the studio.
    siteSettings,
//insert two rows here
    event,
    venue,
    ...
])
```

Deploying the schema

To view the schema changes, they must be deployed. When we deploy something, we
move or copy it from one environment to another, usually a production environment
where it can be used by other people and things. Here, we will push our changes to the
schema into an environment where they may be viewed in the browser. In the root of the
project directory, use either npm or yarn to install the dependencies.

Execute one of the following commands by typing it in the Terminal and pressing *Enter*:

```
yarn install
```

or

```
npm install
```

Once `yarn` or `npm` is used, usually it is beneficial to continue using one or the other, but not both.

Then, start up the development version of Sanity and Gatsby. Execute one of the following commands by typing it in the Terminal and pressing *Enter*:

```
yarn run dev
```

or

```
npm run dev
```

Using Lerna

Lerna, a tool used to manage projects with multiple packages, is used to run both Sanity and Gatsby at the same time. Here is how it works:

There is a `package.json` file in the root folder of the project. Running the `npm run dev` command will, in turn, execute the following code:

```
"scripts": {
  ...
  "dev": "lerna run dev --parallel",
  ...
```

This command, `npm run dev`, is an alias for `lerna run dev –parallel`.

Lerna uses the `lerna.json` file in the root folder of the project. The packages that it will reference are web and `studio`, which correspond to the project's two folders:

```
{
  "packages": [
    "web",
    "studio"
  ],
  "version": "1.0.0"
}
```

Likewise, in the web folder, the relevant line in the `package.json` file is the following:

```
"dev": "npm run clean-cache && gatsby develop",
```

The dev alias will be called, which in turn deletes the cache, and then gatsby develop, which starts up the Gatsby development environment.

In the studio folder, which is the focus of this chapter, the relevant line in the package.json file is the following:

```
"dev": "sanity start",
```

Similarly, the dev alias will be called, which in turn, calls sanity start, which starts up the Sanity development environment. The schema files will be now applied locally, so a local version of Sanity Studio may be accessed at https://localhost:3333.

This will be accessed through a web browser. The two new schemas – **Event** and **Venue** – that we've added should now be visible in the left menu as shown in the following figure:

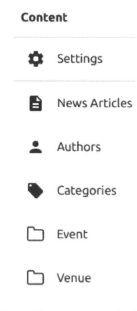

Figure 4.3 – Content navigation

The **Add new event** screen can now be seen by following the method in the previous chapter.

The following screenshot is an example of the **Add new event** screen. Take note of the radio button for **Virtual Event**, which automatically gets created from the Boolean value specified in the schema:

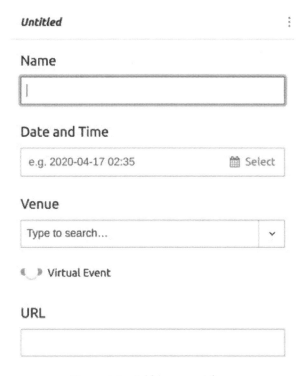

Figure 4.4 – Add new event form

Similarly, an example of the **Venue** screen is shown. Notice the **Location** input, which is a `geopoint`:

Figure 4.5 – Add Venue form

Summary

In this chapter, we learned about schemas: how they are constructed and how to create new schemas. Then, we learned how to start up the Sanity and Gatsby development environments to visualize the schema changes in a local development version of Sanity Studio. These are the basic steps that can be repeated many times, adding to and modifying the schema as needed, and subsequently viewing the website as it begins to take form.

In the next chapter, we will introduce GROQ, Sanity's open source query language, and learn how it compares with the **Standard Query Language** (**SQL**). We will learn the basic syntax, practice some basic queries, and then learn how to do advanced joins.

5
Sanity's GROQ Language

In this chapter, we are going to explore GROQ, Sanity's open source query language. We will learn why GROQ was created and how to use GROQ and the Vision plugin to interact with our Sanity Studio dataset. We will also do a comparison between GROQ and SQL, and after that, we will run basic and advanced queries with GROQ.

By learning what GROQ is and how to use it, we can then quickly begin to use it to write custom queries to obtain filtered and sorted data.

We will cover the following topics in this chapter:

- Why GROQ?
- GROQ versus SQL
- Basic queries with GROQ
- Advanced GROQ

Technical requirements

A web browser and terminal emulator are needed for this chapter.

The code files for this chapter are placed at `https://github.com/PacktPublishing/Jumpstart-Jamstack-Development/tree/chapter_five`.

Why GROQ?

The datastore is the most important part of what *defines* Sanity. Sanity is built for structured content, which is richer than simple two-dimensional tables. Likewise, GROQ is meant to be more powerful and easier to use than traditional SQL, used to query a database. **GROQ** stands for **Graph Oriented Query** language, so, as the name suggests, it is a query language used to query graphs, which are able to represent more complex data structures.

GROQ has four main features:

- **Expressive filtering**: This allows us to build the query using a speakable syntax. If we are looking for a `venue` within our venues named `Will's Pub`, then we will simply use the following expression, which equates to *where* the `type` is `venue` and the (venue) name is `Will's Pub`:

```
_type== "venue" && name=="Will's Pub"
```

- **Joins**: GROQ can join together several documents, combining the result together.
- **Shaping**: You can decide which content fields to include or also rename the field names, reformat the resulting data structure, and even do additional filters within a projection using the values of the parent document.

  Even though this way of obtaining information is quite a paradigm shift for many database developers who are familiar with SQL databases, with experience GROQ can become very easy to use. Additionally, since GROQ is open source, all the code can be examined.

- **Compactness**: GROQ is more compact and less verbose than standard SQL. The syntax is terser in most cases – just as ES6 is terser than ES5.

Sanity Studio's toolbar is displayed at the top of the page found at `http://localhost:3333` by typing the following command in the terminal while in the `studio` directory:

```
sanity start
```

Two of the main tools – the **Dashboard** and **Desk** are automatically installed. To be able to try out GROQ with actual queries against a dataset, we will install a third tool, called **Vision**. Vision gives us a way to type in queries and instantly view the resulting dataset, optionally filtered and sorted. This will help us use GROQ inside of code.

Installing Vision

To install Vision, take the following steps and use the terminal command line:

1. Inside the `studio` folder, type the following command:

```
sanity install @sanity/vision
```

Upon successful installation, the **Vision** icon should be visible together with the other tools in your local Sanity Studio application:

Figure 5.1 – The top navigation

2. Click on the **Vision** icon and a screen will appear that will allow the user to execute GROQ queries:

Figure 5.2 – The Vision screen for GROQ queries

In the top navigation, the **DATASET** selector allows the user to select which dataset to use. The light-blue **Run query** button will perform the query. The **Listen** button will activate a mode where changes in the documents from the filter part of your GROQ query are output in real time in the **RESULT** section.

The main body of the screen is divided into three sections. It is very easy to imagine what each section is used for:

- **QUERY** is where the GROQ query will be entered.

- **PARAMS** is where parameter sets that will be passed into the GROQ query can be entered.

- **RESULT** is where the result will be displayed in JSON format. The results may then be expanded or collapsed so that the user can see the overview as well as details.

We have learned how to install the Vision GROQ tool and how to use it. In the next section, we will examine GROQ and compare it to SQL.

GROQ versus SQL

The compactness of GROQ simply uses an initial asterisk sign to denote `select all documents`, and not a single table by default as in standard SQL. While SQL is a traditional schema database, which means you have to decide the structure of your database in advance, divided into tables. Before storing any data, a programmer must define a table, names, and types of columns inside that table. When adding data to a schema database, a programmer must pass the data in the format declared on each column, any extra data or data not matching the format will not be stored in the database.

Sanity's content model is a schema-less database which means you don't need to define tables and columns. The system stores data as key/value pairs or JSON, basically a one-column table. A programmer will be able to add any data in any format into the database, change the existing data, from a Boolean to a string, for example, and add new data types without declaring a new column.

Now let's explore the differences when querying SQL and GROQ:

SQL	GROQ
`select * from table;`	`*`
`select * from content_table where type="movie";`	`*[_type == "movie"]`

A traditional SQL-based database query should have the following syntax:

```
select * from table;
```

Let's look at GROQ:

```
*
```

SQL:

```
select * from content_table where type="movie";
```

GROQ:

```
*[_type == "movie"]
```

Notice that GROQ uses the double equals sign, which resembles a conditional if.

Here's the code to find all the content that is a movie or a book:

SQL:

```
select * from content_table where type in ("movie", "book");
```

GROQ:

```
*[_type in ["movie", "book"]]
```

Notice that GROQ does not require the where keyword. Also, GROQ uses square brackets to represent an array of values.

SQL:

```
select * from content_table where match(`text`) against("love")
and type = "movie";
```

GROQ:

```
*[text match "love" && _type == "movie"]
```

Notice that GROQ uses the double ampersand.

SQL:

```
select * from content_table where type = "movie" order by
created_at ASC LIMIT 10;
```

GROQ:

```
*[_type == "movie"] | order(_createdAt asc) [0..9]
```

SQL:

```
select * from content_table where type = "movie" order by
created_at DESC LIMIT 1;
```

GROQ:

```
*[_type == "movie"] | order(_createdAt desc) [0]
```

The underscores here are from the convention that Sanity uses to mark their *internal* fields required by the datastore.

If you use GROQ against another data source, you may encounter other conventions. GROQ uses zero-based indexing regarding `order by`. GROQ uses Unix-style pipeline notation to combine operations.

In the next section, we are going to execute basic GROQ queries and we are going to explore the structure of the results.

Basic queries with GROQ

In this section, we are going to perform project-related GROQ queries. GROQ syntax can be used to interact with Sanity's API. Additionally, many of Sanity's integrations will be able to obtain information using this syntax.

Selecting all events

The first simple query we are going to run will select all events stored in the dataset.

By default, GROQ will set the order of the results to the id field. The id used in Sanity is the `_id` key in the resulting array:

```
*[_type == "event"]
```

This query will return all event content in a JSON-formatted array as shown:

```
"result":[
  0:{
    "_createdAt":"2020-04-15T22:17:50Z"
    "_id":"6ddd2730-9aca-46dd-a7fd-850ab306f7fb"
    "_rev":"JmIGD46Mad7O6ByZXl1tpF"
    "_type":"event"
    "_updatedAt":"2020-04-27T15:45:45Z"
    "body":[
      0:{...}
    ]
    "dateAndTime":"2020-04-16T22:00:00.000Z"
```

```
    "name":"IT Conference"
    "venue":{
        "_ref":"65929c5e-f2df-4483-b2e4-4f10a654adf8"
        "_type":"reference"
    }
}
1:{...}
2:{...}
]
```

Note that the results are wrapped in `result`. They are represented by a zero-based array and there are three results, so 0, 1, and 2.

Notice that the id is a **Universally Unique Identifier** (**UUID**). This allows for the document to be unique throughout the entire dataset, unlike a database table index, which gets indexed starting with 1, but it is only unique within that single table.

The `_rev` key is the identifier of the revision, or version, of this document.

Since venue is a related document, the `_ref` is the reference to the `_id` of the document. Note that venue is nested and represents a complete document.

Selecting all upcoming events

In this query, we are going to select all upcoming events by adding the dateAndTime condition:

```
*[_type == "event" && dateAndTime >= now()] | order
(dateAndTime asc)
```

We pass the current date value using the now() function, which returns the current date. We could also have passed the dateAndTime value as a string with the YYYY-MM-DD format.

We are also ordering the result by date. We will show all upcoming events starting from the closest event.

Selecting all past events

As for upcoming events, we are using the `now()` function to get the current date value and get all past events:

```
*[_type == "event" && dateAndTime < now()]| order (dateAndTime asc)
```

It will order the results by date starting from the closest.

Selecting upcoming virtual conference and non-virtual conferences

Our previous query returned all events by date but was not filtered by the `Virtual Conference` field. Our `Virtual Conference` field in the `Event` schema is a Boolean. We can add the condition to our GROQ query setting `virtual == true` if the event is virtual or `virtual == false` if the event is not virtual:

- **Select virtual events**:

```
*[_type == "event" && dateAndTime >= now() && virtual == true] | order (dateAndTime asc)
```

- **Select non-virtual events**:

```
*[_type == "event" && dateAndTime >= now() && virtual == false] | order (dateAndTime asc)
```

We have seen how to select all of the fields from the dataset schema. Next, we will learn how to select specific fields to make the result size smaller.

Selecting specific event fields

The results will depend on where we show the content. We may not need all the fields, but rather only certain fields. With this query, we receive only the `name`, `dateAndTime`, and `body` fields for all upcoming events.

We pass the field names in the projection:

```
*[_type == "event" && dateAndTime >= now()] | order (dateAndTime asc) | {name, dateAndTime, body}
```

The result will be the following:

```
"result":[
  0:{
    "body":[
      0:{...}5 items
    ]
    "dateAndTime":"2020-04-24T23:30:00.000Z"
    "name":"The Appleseed Cast"
  }
]
```

We have learned how to select fields from simple queries. Next, we will learn how to work with fields when using relationships between one schema and another.

Selecting specific fields from relationships

In the previous query, we retrieved certain fields from the event content. In this example, we are going to retrieve the venue name and website from the venue content.

In this query, we are going to add the venue fields in the projection:

```
*[_type == "event" && dateAndTime >= "2020-04-24"] | order
(dateAndTime asc) | {name, dateAndTime, body, venue-
>{name,website}}
```

The result will be as follows:

```
"result":[
  0:{
    "body":[
      0:{...}
    ]
    "dateAndTime":"2020-04-24T23:30:00.000Z"
    "name":"The Appleseed Cast"
    "venue":{
      "name":"Will's Pub"
      "website":"https://willspub.com"
    }
  }
]
```

Now that we have covered some basic queries, let's go through more advanced GROQ queries.

Advanced GROQ

In this section, we will see how to get fields from relations, how to create our own formatted response, and finally, we will explore some built-in functions.

Getting events by venues

On a venue page, we want to select all events at that particular venue:

```
*[_type == "event" && venue->name == "Will's Pub"]{
    name,
    venue->{name}
}
```

The result will be as follows:

```
[
    {
        "name": "The Appleseed Cast",
        "venue": {
            "name": "Will's Pub"
        }
    },
    {
        "name": "Friday Drinks",
        "venue": {
            "name": "Will's Pub"
        }
    }
]
```

Not that the venue, Will's Pub, shows results for two events.

Formatting the response

By default, the field name is the response keys field. Sometimes you may need to override the labels. This can be achieved by setting the field key in the projection:

```
*[_type == "event" && venue->name == "Will's Pub"]{
    "eventName": name,
    "venueName": venue->name
}
```

The result will be as follows:

```
"result":[
  0:{
      "eventName":"The Appleseed Cast"
      "venueName":"Will's Pub"
    }
]
```

Notice that the eventName and venueName labels differentiate between the two fields, both called name.

Count result

The count function will simply count the number of results:

```
count(*[_type == "event" && venue->name == "Will's Pub"]{
    "eventName": name,
    "venueName": venue->name
})
```

I have two events created in the venue Will's Pub so the result will be as follows:

```
2
```

2 is the count of the number of events.

Summary

In this chapter, we learned how to use GROQ and how it's a concise, compact way to query a dataset. We learned how it is different than SQL and how it can flatten and shape the query results.

In the next chapter, we'll begin our journey into GraphQL, which is a more universal way to *expose* or *present* Sanity's dataset as an API, meaning that many different static site generators may easily interact with it.

6
Sanity's GraphQL Playground

This chapter introduces GraphQL, a powerful query language. Sanity's GraphQL API enables external programs to interact with its structured content while following the standard that it provides. This allows developers to leverage the rich GraphQL ecosystem of tools and practices that are available in the development community. Both GraphQL and GROQ, which is Sanity's proprietary query language, are open source and can be used to interact with Sanity. However, while GROQ is specific to Sanity, GraphQL is universally used by many applications.

In this chapter, we will explain what GraphQL is, examine some of the basic queries and their format, introduce Sanity's GraphQL Playground, and learn how to use it to create and test GraphQL queries. In this chapter, we will cover the following topics:

- An introduction to GraphQL
- GROQ versus GraphQL
- Sanity.io's GraphQL playground basics

Technical requirements

A web browser and a Terminal program are required.

An introduction to GraphQL

First, let's start by learning about GraphQL. From the GraphQL website, we learn that GraphQL allows its user to describe the data. This means defining how a data structure should be formed. Consider the following example:

```
type Event {
    name: String
    date: Date
}
```

Here, we define the structure of an event. Using GraphQL, we could query the data structure as follows:

```
{
    event(name: "Saturday Night Party") {
        date
    }
}
```

Notice that the basic structure looks almost the same. We are asking for the data to be in the same format as it is defined. The returned data would be in the following format:

```
{
    "event" {
        date: "2020-10-01"
    }
}
```

> **Note:**
> For more information on GraphQL's syntax and specification, please visit
> `http://spec.graphql.org/draft/`.

GraphQL's strength is that it gives its users the ability to request specific information and to obtain predictable results that mirror those requests.

In the following sections, we will learn about why GraphQL is a compact and efficient standard making it useful to obtain data from many data sources such as Sanity.

We will continue our journey into the world of GraphQL by deploying the GraphQL schema and using Sanity's command-line deployment tool.

Deploying the GraphQL API

Since Sanity uses GROQ internally, the optional GraphQL API needs to be deployed if Sanity's dataset is used by other applications. To perform this, we need to return to the command line in the project's `studio` directory.

The following command needs to be typed into the Terminal:

```
sanity graphql deploy
```

We need to install the Sanity command-line program. Please type the following into the command line if it has not been installed already:

```
npm install -g @sanity/cli
```

You will be asked the following question:

```
Do you want to enable a GraphQL playground? (Y/N)
```

At this prompt, simply pressing the *Enter* key, or typing in *Y*, will enable the playground. The last line of the output that is produced should display the playground's browser:

```
GraphQL API deployed to:
https://abcd1234.api.sanity.io/v1/graphql/production/default
```

This URL can be opened in the web browser. Let's examine the format.

Notice that the URL is composed of the following: the project ID (which is shown here as `abcd1234`), followed by `api.sanity.io`, `v1` (version one), `graphql`, the dataset name (in this example, `production`), and, finally, the schema name (in this case, `default`).

In the next section, we will explore the basic syntax of GraphQL.

Basic GraphQL syntax

While Sanity's GROQ uses a more compact syntax, its aim is to effectively get what you need from a collection of data. GraphQL's aim is to allow the requesting service to specify the format of the data in an expressive and typed way to be returned, and then return it in that same format. We will now look at the basic syntax of a GraphQL query and how useful it might be to obtain data easily.

There are two basic types of queries:

- The `all` prefix followed by the schema, `name`, as shown in the following, is used to return multiple records.

- The single-record query, which will return only one record.

Let's start by learning about the `all` query format.

GraphQL's all query

Consider the following example query:

```
{
  allEvent {
    name
  }
}
```

The preceding query will return the name for all of the events in our dataset. The singular form of event is used here instead of the plural form. The result will be in the same format as the query. Notice that the results are wrapped in a data object. Additionally, the `allEvent` query is repeated in the result, and the result is in the same format as the query:

```
{
  "data": {
    "allEvent": [
      {
        "name": "IT Conference"
      },
      ...
    ]
  }
}
```

Next, let's learn about the single-record GraphQL query.

GraphQL's single-record query

The second type of GraphQL query will return only one record. The following snippet is an example of this second type of query:

```
{
    Event(id: "6ddd2730-9aca-46dd-a7fd-850ab306f7fb"){
        name
    }
}
```

Notice that this type of single-record query needs an argument to identify the record. In this case, the id parameter of the event is used.

This will return a single event. The result is in the same format as the query. Notice that the Event query is repeated in the results:

```
{
    "data": {
        "Event": {
            "name": "IT Conference"
        }
    }
}
```

Now that we have learned about the basic syntax of GraphQL, let's delve more deeply into it. In the next section, we'll view the difference between GROQ and GraphQL.

GROQ versus GraphQL

In *Chapter 5*, *Sanity's GROQ Language*, in the *Advanced GROQ* section, we wrote a GROQ query that returned all of the events for a particular venue. Now we will compare GROQ with GraphQL.

Recalling the GROQ syntax, the desired venue was named Will's Pub:

```
*[_type == "event" && venue->name == "Will's Pub"]{
    name,
    venue->{name}
}
```

Next, let's write the corresponding GROQ query in GraphQL:

```
{
  allEvent(where:
  { venue:
    { name:
      { eq:
    "Will's Pub"
      }
    }
  }
)
  {
    name
    venue {
      name
    }
  }
}
```

GROQ's type == "event" equates to allEvent, which is a function. Note that the GraphQL uses SQL's familiar where keyword, which is a parameter. This is then followed by an object as an argument, which is venue. Here, the venue's name parameter is nested within venue. Then, eq is the two-letter abbreviation for equals.

This concludes the function-argument-parentheses set. Then, between curly braces, we list the fields that we are interested in returning. Notice that GraphQL does not use commas between each value, while GROQ does. We return the event name (name) and also the venue name, which, again, is nested.

The result is as follows:

```
{
  "data": {
    "allEvent": [
      {
        "name": "The Appleseed Cast",
        "venue": {
```

```
                "name": "Will's Pub"
          }
     },
     {
          "name": "Friday Drinks",
          "venue": {
               "name": "Will's Pub"
          }
     }
   ]
  }
}
```

As you can see, two events are returned. If only the event, named The Appleseed
Cast, should be returned, an additional argument to the where keyword can be added.
There will be a comma separator. Note that this is the event name, not the venue name, as
both fields had the same name:

```
{
   allEvent(where: { venue: { name: { eq: "Will's Pub" } },
                name: { eq: "The Appleseed Cast" }
} ) {
      name
      venue {
         name
      }
   }
}
```

The result will now still be a list (that is, an array) because allEvent is used; however,
the list will only have one value:

```
{
   "data": {
      "allEvent": [
         {
            "name": "The Appleseed Cast",
            "venue": {
```

```
            "name": "Will's Pub"
          }
        }
      ]
    }
  }
```

This will be important to remember later, as the results will be handled as if there is more than one result.

In the next section, we will use the Sanity.io playground to run GraphQL queries against our Studio application.

GraphQL playground basics

In *Chapter 5, SSanity's GROQ Language*, in the *Installing Vision* section, Sanity's Vision tool was used to test the GROQ queries. Likewise, Sanity uses the GraphQL playground so that we can test GraphQL and interact with its datasets.

The GraphQL playground allows users to create and run GraphQL queries that can later be used to obtain information from a GraphQL API. In the following section, we will learn about its basic functionality.

The following is a screenshot of the GraphQL playground:

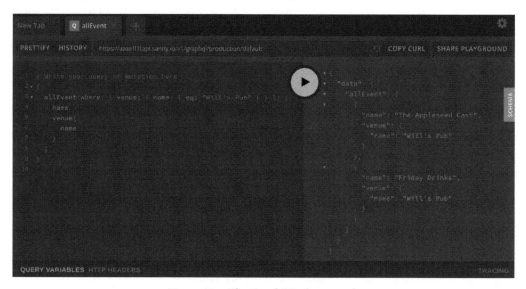

Figure 6.1 – The GraphQL playground

The GraphQL playground's interface is easy to use. Similar to the Vision GROQ tool, the queries are typed into the left-side window and are executed by clicking on the *play* icon in the middle of the interface.

As expected, the GraphQL results are displayed in the right window. Query variables may be entered into a bottom window.

On the right, there is a green-colored tab, labeled **SCHEMA**. Clicking on this will reveal the various GraphQL starting points, such as `allEvent`. Navigating through this schema is a convenient way to determine whether the GraphQL was deployed correctly after typing in the Sanity `graphql deploy` command. This command is required after any changes to the schema are made in Sanity.

If a schema or schema field is not viewable here, then it will not be accessible to any external service that uses this API, so it's a convenient way to check that the schema reflects the actual state of the dataset. In the following code block, a basic query format is displayed, together with the type of value expected for each parameter:

```
allEvent(
   where: EventFilter
   sort: [EventSorting!]
   limit: Int
   offset: Int
): [Event!]!
```

This is how it might look on the screen upon clicking on the `allEvent` link:

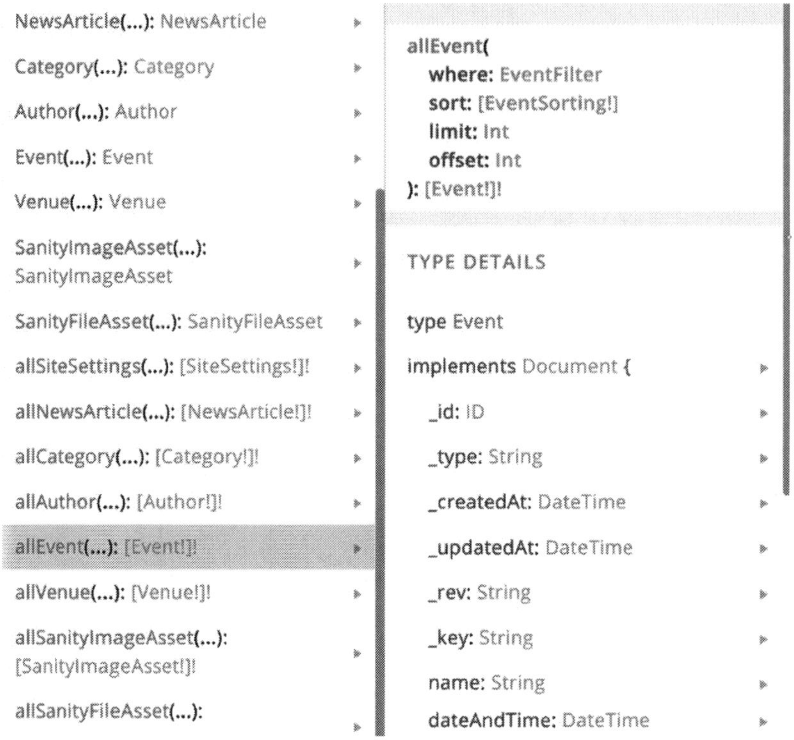

NewsArticle(...): NewsArticle	▸
Category(...): Category	▸
Author(...): Author	▸
Event(...): Event	▸
Venue(...): Venue	▸
SanityImageAsset(...): SanityImageAsset	▸
SanityFileAsset(...): SanityFileAsset	▸
allSiteSettings(...): [SiteSettings!]!	▸
allNewsArticle(...): [NewsArticle!]!	▸
allCategory(...): [Category!]!	▸
allAuthor(...): [Author!]!	▸
allEvent(...): [Event!]!	▸
allVenue(...): [Venue!]!	▸
allSanityImageAsset(...): [SanityImageAsset!]!	▸
allSanityFileAsset(...):	▸

```
allEvent(
    where: EventFilter
    sort: [EventSorting!]
    limit: Int
    offset: Int
): [Event!]!
```

TYPE DETAILS

type Event

implements Document {   ▸

  _id: ID   ▸

  _type: String   ▸

  _createdAt: DateTime   ▸

  _updatedAt: DateTime   ▸

  _rev: String   ▸

  _key: String   ▸

  name: String   ▸

  dateAndTime: DateTime   ▸

Figure 6.2 – allEvent details

Query parameters

One of the most important features of the GraphQL playground is its ability to allow the user to add parameters. This is because, in most real-world applications, query parameters will be often used to obtain the correct results. Expand on the **QUERY VARIABLES** window by dragging it with the mouse. Then, you can enter in key and value pairs, as follows:

```
{"name": "Will's Pub"}
```

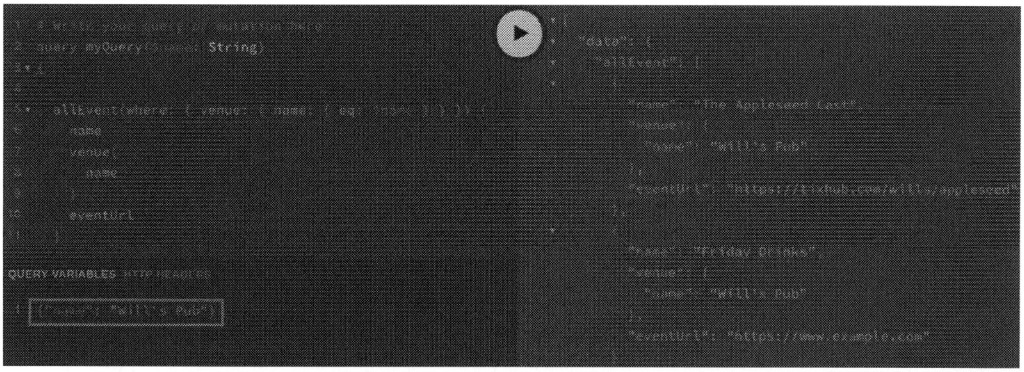

Figure 6.3 – The Sanity playground's query parameters

Then, the parameter may be used as follows:

```
query myQuery($name: String)
{

  allEvent(where: { venue: { name: { eq: $name } } }) {
    name
    venue{
      name
    }
    eventUrl
  }
}
```

The name is passed into the query function, arbitrarily myQuery, in this scenario. Note that the parameter uses a dollar sign prefix. Then, after the colon, the string is used to specify which type of value will be passed into the function. Then, $name is used in place of Will's Pub for the expression "the venue name equals...". Modeling parameter passing is useful for testing.

Summary

In this chapter, we learned how GraphQL is formed, how GraphQL differs from GROQ, and how to filter results using `where`. Finally, we learned how to use Sanity's GraphQL playground to construct and verify the schemas, and we looked at examples. GraphQL will be the means by which all programs wishing to connect to Sanity might easily do so in a standard and compact way. In the following chapters, GraphQL will be important since the static-site generator will use it exclusively.

In the next chapter, we will introduce Gatsby, another part of the Jamstack. We will use some of the GraphQL examples shown here in order to connect Sanity's datasets to Gatsby.

7
Gatsby – An Introduction

Gatsby is the second part of the three-part Jamstack system used in this book. The definition that Gatsby gives for itself is as follows:

> *"A free and open source framework based on React that helps developers build blazing fast websites and apps."*

Since it is a free and open source framework, all of the code is easily examined and modifiable. Secondly, the websites and apps that Gatsby produces are blazing fast because the HTML pages that it creates are actual files, and not just produced through backend processes written in server-side languages.

First, we'll learn what React is, then, we will look at how Gatsby's basic project is structured, examining its file and folder structure.

The main topics that we will cover in this chapter are as follows:

- Gatsby, built on React
- Gatsby basic project structure
- The `gatsby develop` command

Technical requirements

For this chapter, the Gatsby application needs to be installed, and a Terminal program and a web browser are required.

Gatsby, built on React

React is a JavaScript library used to create user interfaces. It uses declarative syntax and also a modular component-based system. Since Gatsby is built on top of React, you will quickly discover many pieces of React as you learn more about Gatsby. Another part of the Gatsby ecosystem called **JSX** is also used by Gatsby. JSX allows Gatsby page elements to be written using the familiar HTML tag format and allows the use of attributes to pass parameters to them. Each JSX tag can be a single unit of a project. Since JSX tags are also JavaScript, they may be integrated with JavaScript programming logic.

Since React is one of many JavaScript libraries and frameworks, such as Angular and Vue, the framework itself is quite large, with a healthy ecosystem, and much learning is required to develop proficiency. Luckily, there are many training courses specific to React should you want to more deeply learn how to use it. While learning React is outside of the scope of this book, learning Gatsby will indirectly expose you to some of React's ways of doing things.

Gatsby basic project structure

In this project, the project's files were created through `https://create.sanity.io`. During the creation process, Gatsby's project file structure and configuration were automatically installed directly in the `/web` folder, and this is roughly equivalent to what would be installed using Gatsby's new project creation command.

If Gatsby was created using the `-g` flag, which signifies globally, it gets installed and becomes available system-wide to the user:

```
npm install -g gatsby
```

Otherwise, Gatsby commands can be run in the directory where it was installed according to the `package.json` file.

A new project can be created, alternatively, by typing the following command in the Terminal:

```
gatsby new projectname
```

In the preceding example, `projectname` is the name of your chosen project and will also become the name of the folder created wherever the command is typed.

We'll take a closer look at the file structure of our project in the following sections.

gatsby-config.js

The first file that we will learn about is `gatsby-config.js`. This file is installed in the `/web` folder.

Next, we'll look at the three main points of the file:

- Its structure
- Its syntax
- Gatby's Sanity installation

Let's begin.

Structure

The file begins with `module.exports`, which is a Node.js way of allowing the contents of the curly braces to be exposed and used in (that is, exported to) other parts of the application:

```
module.exports = {}
```

The main part of the file is `siteMetadata`, which holds the application's metadata, such as `title` and `description`, and `plugins`, which is an array of plugins, represented syntactically by square parentheses. An excerpt of the `gatsby-config.js` file is shown:

```
module.exports = {
  siteMetadata: {
    title: `Gatsby Default Starter`,
    description: `Kick off your next, great Gatsby project with
this default starter...`,
    author: `@gatsbyjs`,
  },
  plugins: [
    `gatsby-plugin-react-helmet`,
    {
      resolve: `gatsby-source-filesystem`,
```

```
    options: {
        name: `images`,
        path: `${__dirname}/src/images`,
      },
    },
    ...
  ],
}
```

Next, we'll look at the syntax of the file.

Syntax

You may not be familiar with the syntax used throughout Gatsby:

```
path: `${__dirname}/src/images`,
```

This syntax, called a **template literal**, is part of ECMAScript 2015, or ES6, the latest JavaScript specification. The backtick character is used here, where previously, single quotation marks would often have been used.

One disadvantage to single quotation marks is that they are not multi-line, so for example, a plus sign is needed to concatenate, or combine sequentially, the two phrases. Here is an example:

```
var multilineString = 'This is an example of a ' +
' multi-line string that is more than one line long.';
```

In ES6, the equivalent can be achieved with the following:

```
let multilineString = `This is an example of a
multi-line string that is more than one line long.`
```

Additionally, the let keyword is used in place of the var keyword. Whereas previously, only a variable (var) could be declared, now let can be used to assign a value that can change. The constant (const) keyword can be used to designate a value that cannot change, meaning that it is immutable.

Additionally, string interpolation is achieved by enclosing a variable in curly braces (also called curly brackets) and then preceding it with a dollar sign ($). This allows using both variables and simply strings within the same expression as shown:

```
path: `${__dirname}/src/images`,
```

Here, the __dirname variable will be replaced with the name of the directory. See the following example:

```
path: `/home/chris/src/images`
```

Finally, let's learn how to configure Gatsby to work with Sanity.

Sanity's Gatsby installation

Since the version of Gatsby used in the book was installed and configured based on the instructions at https://www.sanity.io/create, it is preconfigured to work with Sanity, even though Gatsby may obtain and use information from many different types of information sources. This happens through Gatsby's source plugins, which are named in the following format:

```
gatsby-source-name
```

The name value in the preceding snippet could be replaced with Sanity (gatsby-source-sanity), WordPress (gatsby-source-wordpress), Drupal (gatsby-source-drupal), or any of hundreds of different types of data sources at the time of writing this book. The default Gatsby source is gatsby-source-filesystem. In *Chapter 9, Gatsby Source Plugins*, we will discuss this in more detail.

This is an example of the gatsby-source-sanity plugin. It has a list of options:

```
{
    resolve: "gatsby-source-sanity",
    options: {
        ...clientConfig.sanity,
        token: process.env.SANITY_READ_TOKEN,
        watchMode: !isProd,
        overlayDrafts: !isProd
    }
}
```

The first thing to notice is the following line:

```
...clientConfig.sanity,
```

The triple period is used in JavaScript as the spread operator, which assigns all the object attributes into separate variables. But first, let's examine what happens beforehand.

The first few lines of this configuration file are important:

```
// Load variables from `.env` as soon as possible
require('dotenv').config({
    path: `.env.${process.env.NODE_ENV || 'development'}`
})
const clientConfig = require('./client-config')
const isProd = process.env.NODE_ENV === 'production'
```

These lines are important because they determine Gatsby's environment variables and set up the Sanity integration. An environment variable is a variable whose value can vary depending on the environment in which it is used.

For example, in production, an email may be sent after completing a form, whereas in the development environment, it would not be sent.

dotenv

The dotenv file is a convention used to store configuration values. It is usually not committed to source code control, GitHub in this case, so that credentials and passwords may be kept private:

```
require('dotenv').config({
    path: `.env.${process.env.NODE_ENV || 'development'}`
})
```

There is an example of this file in the /web directory, namely .env.production, with the following format:

```
GATSBY_SANITY_PROJECT_ID="abcd1234"
GATSBY_SANITY_DATASET="production"
```

`process.env.NODE_ENV` is used to determine which environment is currently being used. `development` is the default environment used if none is specified, so to enable this file to be used, it must exist in the correct format. Create a copy of `.env.production` and name it `env.development`. The `.env.production` file will be used for production deployments.

Client configuration

The next line requires loading the contents of the `client-config` file, meaning that it must bring its contents into the current code.

Here are the contents of the file. This is used to set two values, `projectId` and `dataset`. It assigns the values from the `.env` file, if present, or else the actual names provided when the project was created:

```
module.exports = {
  sanity: {
    projectId: process.env.GATSBY_SANITY_PROJECT_ID ||
abcd1234',
    dataset: process.env.GATSBY_SANITY_DATASET || 'production'
  }
}
```

These values get set into the `clientConfig` variable, and then the contents are spread into the `gatsby-source-sanity` options where they are used to connect to the Sanity GraphQL API:

```
options: {
  ...clientConfig.sanity,

const clientConfig = require('./client-config'),
```

At this point, the `clientConfig` constant holds the Sanity configuration.

Next, let's learn about Gatsby's key files.

Key Gatsby files

Three key files in any Gatsby project are `gatsby-ssr.js`, `gatsby-node.js`, and `gatsby-browser.js`. They collectively belong to the Gatsby API. Each file has a particular purpose. Interestingly, each of these files is optional, so they can be created and added to the project as needed.

It's important to learn how the build process works. Remember that since a static site generator literally produces only files, once a web page is produced, it can no longer execute server-side code. All the server-side code execution will occur in a file called `gatsby-ssr.js`.

Let's look at the three key files in detail.

- `gatsby-ssr.js`: **SSR** is an acronym for **server-side rendering**, so it soon becomes clear what the purpose of this file is. This file allows you to modify the content of the pages as they are being generated (rendered) on the server by Gatsby. The functions that can be called from inside of this file will interact with the pages at build time as they are rendered.

- `gatsby-node.js`: Since Gatsby uses Node.js, the functions in this file allow Gatsby to tap into the entire process.

- `gatsby-browser.js`: This is the file where the actual interaction on the page will occur after the web pages are rendered.

Gatsby folders

Here is a list of the main Gatsby folders.

src

This folder contains the Gatsby source files, including images and the cascading style sheets that are used to style the website. Additionally, the following folders are contained within the `src` folder.

- `Components`: In this directory are the building blocks that will be used for website construction. Inside of this directory, there will be pieces of content used across multiple pages.

- `Pages`: The contents of this directory are used for single pages; for example, an *about us* page, where it is the only page of its type. Another example is a 404 page, used when a user enters a web address into the browser address bar that doesn't exist, or clicks a link to a page on the website that doesn't exist either. Each page should have a unique layout. If the pages are too similar, then templates should be used where many of the same types exist, such as for blog articles.

- `Templates`: As mentioned previously, a template is used to create many pages of the same type, where all of the pages for a single template have almost the exact same format and layout, for example, with just the page title, headline, and body content differing.

public

Located outside of the `src` directory, this folder is where the deployed website pages will be created if they do not already exist when `gatsby build` is run in the command line. This is also where the files will be referenced as the document root when a Gatsby website is first viewed using the `gatsby serve` command. The contents of the public directory may be deleted and recreated at any time since running `gatsby build` will always recreate them.

The complete Gatsby documentation may be found at `https://www.gatsbyjs.com/docs/`, and looks as follows:

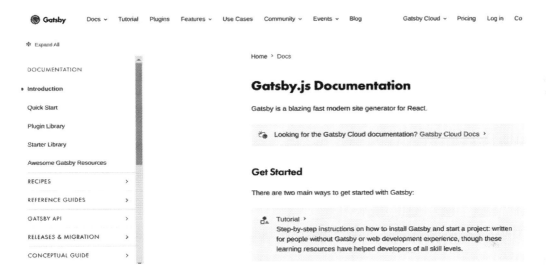

Figure 7.1 – Gatsby website documentation

Now that we've learned about Gatsby's file and folder structure, we will move on to learn how to use Gatsby. To start up Gatsby, we'll need to use the command line. Start Gatsby in development mode.

The gatsby develop command

Using Gatsby at the command line provides many different types of functionality for the various project stages. Initially, the `gatsby develop` command will start up Gatsby in development mode. This allows changes to be viewed in real time. The command won't stop running until you press *Ctrl + C*. This key combination is used in the UNIX operating system to terminate (kill) a process.

From inside the /web directory, type gatsby develop, as this will cause the Gatsby development environment (.env.development) to run, using the development configuration, as opposed to the production configuration (.env.production). Also, it will create a GraphQL playground called **GraphiQL** (pronounced like *graphical*). This will allow us to actually interact with Sanity's GraphQL interface and to begin to write, test, and view the results of the queries needed to create our events website.

Summary

In this chapter, we learned about what Gatsby is and how it is built using JavaScript and React. Next, we learned how its configuration file is created, and what its main parts are. We also learned how to configure the gatsby-source plugin to interact with Sanity. We also learned about the gatsby develop command and how to start up a project.

In the next chapter, we'll begin our journey with GraphiQL, a GraphQL playground, and move closer to creating a website. This will allow us to design, execute, and test GraphQL queries within the Gatsby context.

8
Gatsby and GraphQL

In this chapter, we'll begin to bring content into Gatsby through GraphQL. GraphQL is a good starting point for learning about how Gatsby works, since Gatsby sources content using GraphQL. As we learned in *Chapter 6*, *Sanity's GraphQL Playground*, Sanity exposes its information through a GraphQL **Application Programming Interface** (**API**), so Gatsby can easily use Sanity's content through GraphQL.

These are the main topics that we will cover in this chapter:

- GraphQL in GatsbyJS
- GraphiQL, a GraphQL navigator

Technical requirements

For this chapter, the Gatsby application needs to be installed and a Terminal program is needed. Additionally, a web browser is needed.

GraphQL in GatsbyJS

In this section, we'll learn about how GraphQL is used in the context of Gatsby. We will learn what the major difference is between how GraphQL is used by Gatsby and how it is exposed by Sanity's GraphQL API.

Gatsby's use of GraphQL is different from Sanity's since it uses the concept of a graph to formulate its GraphQL queries. Let's learn what a graph is.

In the following diagram, the figure consists of nodes and edges:

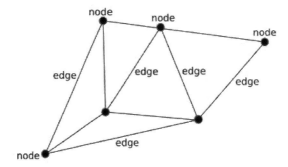

Figure 8.1 – A graph

In Gatsby's implementation of GraphQL, in reference to the graph, each Sanity document is represented as a node. Recalling the GraphQL query that was used in *Chapter 6, Sanity's GraphQL Playground,* to return all events, this query was quite simple, as highlighted in the following code snippet:

```
{
    allEvent {
        name
    }
}
```

In Gatsby, we find that the corresponding query to return all events has two main differences, as follows:

- `allSanityEvent` is used in place of `allEvent`. Sanity's developers created and officially maintain the `gatsby-source-sanity` plugin. They have chosen to add this prefix to differentiate Sanity documents from others, a technique sometimes called **namespacing**. Gatsby endorses this as a good practice. Obviously, using GraphQL Playground on the Sanity side means that only Sanity's content is being sourced, whereas in Gatsby it is possible to use many different content sources at the same time.

- The query needs to specify the edges and node parts to be able to return each event, as shown in the following code example:

```
query MyQuery {
  allSanityEvent {
    edges {
      node {
        name
      }
    }
  }
}
```

Likewise, since GraphQL is specifying not only the request format but also the result format, results are returned encapsulated in an array of edges and a node for each document, as follows:

```
{
  "data": {
    "allSanityEvent": {
```

Likewise, the results of the query also contain the edges and nodes, as shown in the following code snippet:

```
{
  "data": {
    "allSanityEvent": {
      "edges": [
        {
          "node": {
            "name": "The Appleseed Cast"
          }
        },
        {
          "node": {
            "name": "Friday Drinks"
          }
        }
      ],
    }
```

```
        }
    }
```

Now that we've seen the basic difference between how GraphQL is used in both Sanity and Gatsby, we will introduce another application similar to GraphQL Playground, called GraphiQL, to explore and work with GraphQL queries.

GraphiQL, a GraphQL navigator

GraphiQL (pronounced *graphical*) is similar to GraphQL Playground, which we learned about in *Chapter 6, Sanity's GraphQL Playground*. GraphQL Playground uses components of GraphiQL, and in fact, at the time of writing, the two projects are merging and will become one.

As mentioned in *Chapter 7, Gatsby - An Introduction*, by typing the following command from the command line, Gatsby will start an instance of GraphiQL at `http://localhost:8000/graphql`:

```
gatsby develop
```

In the text output from the command, Gatsby will provide the **Uniform Resource Locator** (**URL**). Here is an excerpt of the output:

```
...
View GraphiQL, an in-browser IDE, to explore your site's data
and schema

   http://localhost:8000/___graphql
...
```

By clicking on the `http://localhost:8000/graphql` URL if possible or, optionally, simply typing the URL into the browser, the GraphiQL GraphQL **Integrated Development Environment** (**IDE**) will appear. Notice that there are three underscores after the front slash in the URL. The following screenshot is an example of how the web-based application will appear upon startup. The interface is composed of several distinct areas:

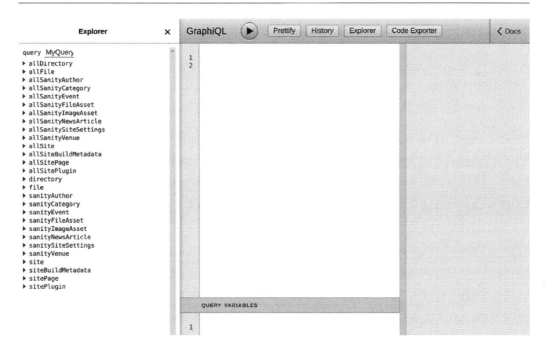

Figure 8.2 – GraphiQL

On the left-hand side, we can see the GraphQL **Explorer**. This helps us to automatically create GraphQL queries by providing the user with a view of all of schemas available for use. So, by expanding each of the schemas, options for filtering and sorting are shown, along with the fields (including their nest elements) that are available to be returned as the query result. Let's look, in detail, at an example similar to what was previously discussed in *Chapter 6*, *Sanity's GraphQL Playground*.

Clicking on the desired starting query—for example, `allSanityEvent`—the various entity fields that may be used for filter options will be seen, and the basic query will be created in the middle section. As the various fields are chosen, GraphiQL will automatically add those fields to the `graphql` query.

Next, let's examine the following screenshot of the expanded `allSanityEvent` section:

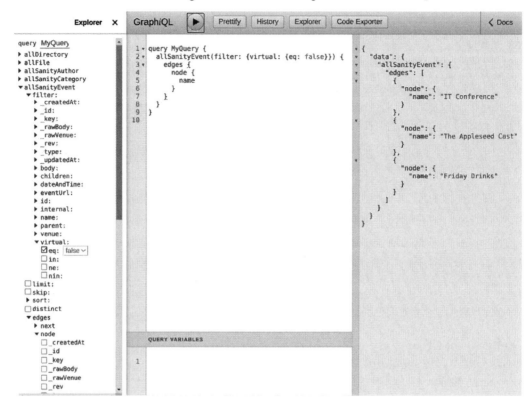

Figure 8.3 – GraphiQL with an example query

As the `allSanityEvent` section is expanded, followed by `filter`, the filter options are shown. `virtual eq false` filters results based on the following criteria: only the events that are not virtual (`eq false`) are selected. The following screenshot shows details of the left-side navigation that allows for the filtering and selection of fields to return from the query:

Figure 8.4 – Query options

Then, `name` is chosen from the list of node fields after expanding `edges`.

The query is automatically created, as follows:

```
query MyQuery {
    allSanityEvent(filter: {virtual: {eq: false}}) {
        edges {
            node {
                name
            }
        }
    }
}
```

To execute the query, click on the **Play** button.

The results are shown in the third panel, on the right-hand side. Two other features are **History** and **Prettify**. **Prettify** is used to properly format the code.

The **History** feature, as the name entails, is used to be able to recall a previous query, as shown in the following screenshot:

Figure 8.5 – GraphiQL's GraphQL query history panel

Possibly the most useful and time-saving feature of GraphiQL, however, is the **Code Exporter**. This feature may be accessed by the **Code Exporter** button, as shown in the following screenshot:

FIgure 8.6 – The GraphiQL button panel

By clicking the **Code Exporter** button, source code will be automatically produced that can be exported and used in a Gatsby project. The following code lines that are produced create a minimal React component for use with Gatsby, based on the content of the query:

```
import React from "react"
import { graphql } from "gatsby"


const ComponentName = ({ data }) => <pre>{JSON.stringify(data,
null, 4)}</pre>
export const query = graphql`
  { allSanityEvent {
    edges {
      node {
```

```
            name
         }
      }
    }
  }
`export default ComponentName
```

Let's examine the code that is generated. The first line imports React. The second line imports `graphql` from `gatsby`, needed to perform the query. Next, we define the component called `ComponentName`, by creating an anonymous function and assigning it to a constant, since the function will not change. In this case, `ComponentName` is a valid name but is meant to be a placeholder that should be changed.

Next, let's examine what a single event query would look like. Instead of `allSanityEvent`, which would return all events from the Sanity side to Gatsby, we will use the single `sanityEvent` event query for GraphQL, which will return just one record, accepting the `id` of the event from the Sanity side, denoted by an underscore. The following code snippet shows an example of this concept:

```
query MyQuery {
    sanityEvent(_id: {eq: "6ddd2730-9aca-46dd-a7fd-
850ab306f7fb"}) {
      name
  }
}
```

Next, let's examine the results. Notice in the following code snippet that the results are wrapped in a `data` object:

```
{
  "data": {
    "sanityEvent": {
      "name": "IT Conference"
    }
  }
}
```

Similarly, we can query an event using the venue name, as shown in the following code snippet. This is similar to the example shown in *Chapter 6, Sanity's GraphQL Playground*:

```
query MyQuery {
    sanityEvent( venue: {name: {eq: "Will's Pub"}}) {
        name
    }
}
```

Similarly, the results will be as shown with the name of the event, as requested in the name field from the preceding code snippet, as follows:

```
    "data": {
        "sanityEvent": {
            "name": "The Appleseed Cast"
    "venue": {
                "name": "Will's Pub"
            }
        }
    }
}
```

These two examples show clearly how GraphQL is used within Gatsby, providing an easy way to query a Sanity source via GraphQL.

Summary

In this chapter, we learned about the Gatsby Sanity source plugin and how it uses GraphQL to interact with and import content from Sanity. We learned how to use GraphQL to test and write GraphQL queries in the context of Gatsby, using the GraphiQL web-based application. We also learned how GraphQL obtains Sanity's content through its GraphQL API.

In the next chapter, we'll learn about how Gatsby can source additional content from sources such as the filesystem and **Content Management Systems (CMS)**, as we move closer to building a website using Gatsby.

9
Gatsby Source Plugins

In this chapter, we are going to explain how to extend the functionalities of Gatsby by using plugins. We will start by exploring the basics of a plugin, and then look at how to install and maintain a plugin. We will explore where to find a plugin and how Gatsby manages its plugins. At the end of the chapter, we will install and configure two new plugins to our Gatsby application.

We will cover the following topics in this chapter:

- Understanding plugins
- Searching, installing, and configuring plugins

Technical Requirements

We will need the following to understand this chapter thoroughly:

- A Terminal application
- npm
- The Gatsby application installed.

The code files for this chapter can be found at `https://github.com/PacktPublishing/Jumpstart-Jamstack-Development/tree/chapter_nine`.

> **Note:**
> The Drupal section is relevant only if you have a Drupal website. GitHub link: `https://github.com/PacktPublishing/Jumpstart-Jamstack-Development/tree/chapter_nine_drupal`.

The Drupal application with the following modules enabled:

- RESTful Web Services
- JSON:API
- Serialization

Understanding plugins

In this section, we will explore the basics of a plugin, what a plugin is, and why it is needed in a project. We will explore the public collection of open source code, npm. We will explain how semantic versioning control works and why it is important. We will then see how to install and maintain plugins.

Gatsby plugins are Node.js packages, a set of JavaScript and **HyperText Markup Language/Cascading Style Sheets** (**HTML/CSS**) files that extend the Gatsby **application programming interfaces** (**APIs**) and add new functionalities to the application. You can enable a feature by installing a plugin, and you can disable it by uninstalling the plugin.

The extensible nature of Gatsby allows you to create your plugins in a way that allows you to organize your customized business logic into reusable packages, discussed in the next section.

Node Package Manager

A developer can download plugins from npm, which is a public collection of open source code for JavaScript frameworks such as GatsbyJS. Developers can upload their plugins and let other developers reuse the same code. Other developers can also contribute back to the plugin they have used by fixing bugs or adding functionalities. You can also upload private packages to npm.

You can search for a plugin on npm from the search tool on the following website:

`https://www.npmjs.com`

On the **package** page on the aforementioned website, you can find the description of a package, with installation instructions, dependencies, and versions. In the next section, we will explore the package versioning method that uses semantic versioning.

Semantic versioning

In software development, developers assign a unique version number to a unique state of the software. Versioning a software helps developers to choose the right version needed to implement their software. This applies to packages, too.

When a package is created and added to npm, the first recommended version is 1.0.0. With further implementation and bug fixing, the version number increments depending on the type of change introduced.

The packages must follow *major.minor.patch* semantic versioning, detailed as follows:

- The *major* version increments by one when a developer introduces incompatible API changes. The version changes from 1.0.0 to 2.0.0.

- The *minor* version increments by one when a developer introduces a backward-compatible new functionality. The version changes from 1.0.0 to 1.1.0.

- The *patch* version increments by one when a developer introduces a backward-compatible bug fix. The version changes from 1.0.0 to 1.0.1.

Next, we will see how to install a package from npm.

Installing a package from npm

To install a package from npm, from your Terminal, run the following command:

```
npm i <package_name>
```

Here, `<package_name>` is the name of the package. For example, if you would like to install a package from npm called `birdie-hop`, you can run the following command on your Terminal:

```
npm i birdie-hop
```

With the preceding command, npm will get the latest stable release of the `birdie-hop` package into your application.

We can also specify the version we want by adding the version to the package name, as shown in the following command:

```
npm i <package_name@version>
```

You may have noticed that I have added @version to the package name. For example, if you want to install version 6.1.46 of the birdie-hop package, you can run the following command on your Terminal:

```
npm i birdie-hop@6.1.46
```

Every time we add a new package, our application keeps track of it inside a package.json file. The new package is listed as a dependency.

Let's explore the package.json file in the next section.

The package.json file

One of the functionalities of the package.json file is to list all the dependencies of a package. It adds the dependencies under the dependencies section when you install a new package.

As you can see in the following example, the package name has been added to the package.json file, along with the version downloaded:

```
...
"dependencies": {
    ...
    "birdie-hop": "^1.2.3",
    ...
    }
...
```

You may have noticed the character before the version number—caret (^), in our case—which tells npm which version to download when we want to install or update the package.

There are two other characters to define version updates: * and ~.

Let's see the difference between these characters. Have a look at the following code snippet:

```
npm i birdie-hop@1.2.3
```

Adding the version with no character before the version will download that exact version if you have never installed the plugin in your app, or it will update the package to that very same version. Now, have a look at this code snippet:

```
npm i birdie-hop@~1.2.3
```

The tilde (~) tells npm that it can install or update the package to the latest patch release available. In this case, the version will be >1.2.3 and <1.3.0. Next, have a look at the following code snippet:

```
npm i birdie-hop@^1.2.3
```

The caret (^) tells npm that it can install or update the package to the latest minor release available. In this case, the version will be >1.2.3 and <2.0.0. Now, have a look at this code snippet:

```
npm i birdie-hop@*1.2.3
```

The asterix (*) tells npm that it can install or update the package to any major version available. In this case, the version will be >1.2.3 and there is no limit on updates. Let's move on to understanding how to update a plugin.

By default, the packages are going under the dependencies array and will be required by your application in production. You can also set up packages that are only needed in your local development environment or on your testing environment, such as automated testing packages. This package will go under the devDependencies array in the packages.json file and can be added by adding the –save-dev flag, as follows:

```
npm i birdie-hop –save-dev
```

Updating a plugin

When a plugin releases an update, we can update our plugin via npm. To update all packages listed in the package.json file, run the following command:

```
npm update
```

To update a single package, run the following command:

```
npm update <package_name>
```

Here, <package_name> is the name of the package you want to update. If you want to update the birdie-hop package, you can run the following command:

```
npm update birdie-hop
```

During updating or installation, npm will check the package.json file and download or update a plugin to the allowed version.

The package.lock file

When you are working in a team, you want all the developers in your team to use the same package versions. In this situation, the package.lock file comes in handy. It is automatically generated when you modify the package.json file or the node_modules folder. It lists all the exact versions of the packages the application should use. The package.lock file will avoid a situation where two developers in the same team working on the same project use two different versions of the birdie-hop package.

In this section, we have explored the main components of a package. We learned where to find the packages and how to install them. We learned about package versioning and how to install and update a specific package to a specific version. We have also explored how package.json and package.lock files play an important role in making sure your application gets the right package with the right version.

In the next section, we will install a package in our Gatsby application.

Searching, installing, and configuring plugins

In this section, we will explore the Gatsby public plugin repository. We will look at how to install a Gatsby plugin and where to find the configuration for the plugins you would like to install.

We will install and configure the gatsby-source-filesystem and gatsby-source-drupal plugins and see how we can use them.

The Gatsby Plugin Library

Gatsby also provides a plugin library, a collection of npm packages tagged with the *Gatsby* keyword. In this library, it is possible to find standard plugins that will be used on most sites, related to **Search Engine Optimization (SEO)**, **Really Simple Syndication (RSS)**, social media buttons, third-party comment services, e-commerce integration, and more.

> **Important note**
> Before you start writing your custom plugin, please make sure it does not already exist in the Gatsby Plugin Library.

There are multiple benefits to using a plugin from the Gatsby Plugin Library. Some of them are listed here:

- **Time-saving**: If a plugin fully accomplishes your task, you can install it, configure it, and start using it. If a plugin partially accomplishes your task, you can extend it by adding your custom functionality on top of it.

- **Bug fixing**: You or other developers may fix bugs and publish the information on npm, and get these fixes by updating the plugin in your application.

- **Improvement**: Same as bug fixing—you or other developers may add new functionality to the plugin and publish it on npm.

- **Security**: You or other developers may find security issues with the code or dependencies in a plugin; update the plugin with the latest security release and publish it on npm.

To find a Gatsby plugin, visit the Gatsby Plugin Library at `https://www.gatsbyjs.org/plugins/`.

The following page provides a **Search Gatsby Library** textbox that lets you navigate through more than 2,000 plugins! The textbox is on the top left-hand side of the page, as illustrated in the following screenshot:

Figure 9.1 – The Gatsby Plugin Library page

Each Gatsby plugin comes with detailed instructions on how to install, configure, and use it. The Gatsby Source plugins allow Gatsby to get the content from a source such as a database, file, RESTful API (where **REST** stands for **REpresentational State Transfer**), and so on.

The `Starter` project that we installed in *Chapter 2, Introduction to Sanity* comes with the `gatsby-source-sanity` plugin already installed and configured. Throughout the `gatsby-source-sanity` plugin, we are able to get content from our Sanity application.

In the following section, we are going to explain how to search for a plugin in the Gatsby Plugin Library. As an example, we are going to install and configure two source plugins: the `gatsby-source-filesystem` and `gatsby-source-drupal` plugins.

Searching for a plugin

All Gatsby plugins can be found in the Gatsby Plugin Library at `https://www.gatsbyjs.org/plugins/`.

On the left-hand side of the page, there is a search tool for a plugin. Start typing the name of a potential keyword for the plugin you are looking for.

For example, if you are looking for the `Google Analytics` plugin, you can type `google analytics`.

In our example, we will look for the `gatsby-source-filesystem` plugin, so we can type `source filesystem`, as shown in the following screenshot:

Figure 9.2 – The Gatsby Plugin Library page

On the left-hand side of the page, it will return all the results containing that keyword. Each result contains the name of the plugin, a description, the number of downloads, and type of plugin. When you click on the plugin result, you will be able to see a description of the plugin and instructions on how to install it.

In the main section of the page, we can now see the name of the plugin, a link to the **GitHub** page, the type of plugin, a link to the **Starter** kits using this plugin, a description of the plugin, and instructions on how it install it, as illustrated in the following screenshot:

Figure 9.3 – The gatsby-source-filesystem plugin page

> **Tip**
>
> When choosing a plugin, click on **View Plugin** on GitHub and check how often it is updated, and check the bugs list under the **Issue** tab to see if there is any conflict with your code base. If you want to try the plugin before you install it in your application, you can install a **Starter** kit that uses that plugin by clicking on **See starters using this**. It will then show a list of Gatsby starters that use that plugin.

Now that we have found the plugin on the Gatsby Plugin Library, let's install it on our application.

Installing and configuring the gatsby-source-filesystem plugin

This plugin gets data into your application from your local or remote filesystem. We will use local Markdown files for this example.

Installing the plugin

Plugins are installed through npm via the command line. When you have found the plugin you are looking for, see the installation command on the plugin page, under the **Install** section, as illustrated in the following screenshot:

Install

```
npm install gatsby-source-filesystem
```

Figure 9.4 – The gatsby-source-filesystem plugin page Install section

Type the command shown in the preceding screenshot in your Terminal inside the web folder of your project, and press *Enter*.

This command will download the plugin and its dependencies inside the node_modules folder and add the gatsby-source-filesystem plugin and version to download in the package.json file, under the **Dependencies** section.

Configuring the plugin

Now, the plugin files are in their own application, but in order to enable a plugin, we need to add it to the gatsby-config.js file located in the root folder of the Gatsby project—in our case, inside the web folder.

The gatsby-config.js file is one of the most important files of the application. It contains configuration for the following:

- siteMetadata (object)
- plugins (array)
- pathPrefix (string)
- polyfill (Boolean)
- mapping (object)
- proxy (object)
- developMiddleware (function)

To enable a plugin, simply add the plugin name in the plugins array in the gatsby-config.js file, like this:

```
module.exports = {
  plugins: [
    ...
```

```
        'gatsby-plugin-name',
        ...
    ]
}
```

Some other plugins may also take configuration options that can be added in the `plugins` array in the `gatsby-config.js` file, as illustrated in the following code snippet:

```
module.exports = {
  plugins: [
    ...
    {
      resolve: 'plugin-name',
      options: {
        // Options list, if any
      },
    },
    ...
  ]
}
```

Now that we know how to enable a plugin, let's enable the `gatsby-source-filesystem` plugin and tell Gatsby where to find our content. On the **Gatsby Plugin** page, under the **How to use** section, there are detailed instructions on how to configure the plugin in your application.

The `gatsby-source-filesystem` plugin can take three options, as follows:

- `name`: The name used by GraphQL queries (*required*)
- `path`: The folder where the actual files live (*required*)
- `ignore`: A list of file extensions to be ignored (*optional*)

In our case, we can add the configuration in this way:

```
module.exports = {
  plugins: [
    ...
    {
      resolve: 'gatsby-source-filesystem',
```

```
        options: {
          path: '${__dirname}/src/data',
          name: 'md-files',
          ignore: ['**/\.*'],
        },
      },
      ...
    ]
}
```

With the preceding code, we enabled the `gatsby-source-filesystem` plugin, and we tell Gatsby where to find the files, the name of our content, and to ignore all files starting with a *dot*. Now, restart your application. From the command line, press *Ctrl + C* and then run the following command:

```
npm run dev
```

As an example, we are going to query data from a Markdown file. We will create a folder called `data` under our `web/src` application folder. Inside the `data` folder, we create all the Markdown files we need. The files are organized in subfolders, and the system will automatically find them. To do that, we need the `gatsby-transformer-remark` plugin, which we are going to install in the next section.

Installing and configuring the gatsby-transformer-remark plugin

This plugin parses and compiles the `Markdown` file and converts it to HTML. It also supports frontmatter so that you can define fields such as `title`, `slug`, `date`, `image`, `excerpt`, and so on.

Let's install and configure the plugin.

Installing the plugin

As this is a Gatsby plugin it can be found in the plugin library, along with installation and configuration instructions.

Inside your `Gatsby` folder, run the following command to install the plugin:

```
npm install --save gatsby-transformer-remark
```

Configuring the plugin

Once the plugin has been downloaded, we are able to enable it by adding only the plugin name in the `gatsby-config.js` file, as shown in the following code block:

```
module.exports = {
  plugins: [
    ...
    'gatsby-transformer-remark',
    ...
  ]
}
```

That's it! Now, restart your application, and we are ready to create our first content!

Creating the content file

In this section, we are going to create our content inside a Markdown file. As we said, `gatsby-transformer-remark` lets you add fields into the `Markdown` file. Let's start adding the frontmatter, as follows:

1. Create a file inside `web/src/data` called `hello-world.md`. At the top and the end of the file, add three dashes. Between those two lines, you can define your frontmatter, as follows:

```
---
// Define your frontmatter.
---
```

2. The fields in the frontmatter can be defined as a key/value pair. We can add the information we want. In this case, we will add `title`, `date`, and `excerpt` in the following way:

```
---
title: Hello World
date: "2020-07-12T09:01:00"
excerpt: Hi! This is my first content from a markdown
file! I will fill with James Joyce's poem.
---
```

3. Now that we have the fields, let's add the body and save the file, like this:

```
---
title: Hello World
date: "2020-07-20T09:01:00"
excerpt: Hi! This is my first content from a markdown
file! I will fill with a James Joyce's poem.
---
# Lean out of the window

> Lean out of the window,
> Goldenhair,
> I hear you singing
> A merry air.
> ...
> Singing and singing
> A merry air,
> Lean out of the window,
> Goldenhair.
```

Our file is now ready to be queried by GraphiQL!

Querying the filesystem with GraphiQL

Now that we have all the plugins, configuration, and content file in the right place, let's start querying the content from our GraphiQL.

Go to `http://localhost:8000/___graphql` and run the following query:

```
query MyQuery {
  allMarkdownRemark {
    edges {
      node {
        frontmatter {
          title
          date
          excerpt
        }
        html
```

```
                }
            }
        }
    }
```

The preceding query will tell GraphQL to retrieve the following fields from the frontmatter section:

- `title`
- `date`
- `excerpt`
- `html`

This query will return the following result:

```
{
    "data": {
        "allMarkdownRemark": {
            "edges": [
                {
                    "node": {
                        "frontmatter": {
                            "title": "Hello World",
                            "date": "2020-07-20T09:01:00",
                            "excerpt": "Hi! This is my first content from a
markdown file! I will fill with a James Joyce poem."
                        },
                        "html": "<h1>Lean out of the window</h1>\
n<blockquote>\n<p>Lean out of the window,\nGoldenhair,\nI hear
you singing\nA merry air.\n...\nSinging and singing\nA merry
air,\nLean out of the window,\nGoldenhair.</p>\n</blockquote>"
                    }
                }
            ]
        }
    }
}
```

As you can see, the frontmatter fields are grouped under the `frontmatter` key, and the rest of the file will be shown as HTML, formatted under the `html` key.

In this section, we have seen how to search, install, and configure Gatsby plugins. As an example, we have used the `gatsby-file-system` and `gatsby-transformer-remark` plugins, we have created a Markdown file, and we have used GraphQL to query our file.

In the next section, we are going to explore how to query another application that uses web services. As an example, we are going to query a Drupal application.

Installing and configuring the gatsby-source-drupal plugin

In this section, we are going to install and configure the `gatsby-source-drupal` plugin. This plugin lets us get content from a Drupal application. Let's first install this plugin.

Installing a gatsby-source-drupal plugin

As with the `gatsby-source-filesystem` and `gatsby-transform-remark` plugins, the `gatsby-source-drupal` plugin can also be found on the Gatsby plugin search page, along with installation and configuration instructions.

To install the latest stable version of the plugin, run the following command from the command line in your Terminal:

```
npm install --save gatsby-source-drupal
```

As usual, the preceding command will download the package into our `nodes_modules` folder.

Configuring the gatsby-source-drupal plugin

Once the module has been installed, as with the previous plugin, we have enabled it, and we need to add the new plugin inside the `plugins` array in the `gatsby-config.js` file.

In this example, we go ahead with the basic configuration, as follows:

```
module.exports = {
  plugins: [
    ...
    {
```

```
        resolve: 'gatsby-source-drupal',
      options: {
        baseUrl: 'site-url', //for example https://example.com
      },
    },
    ...
  ],
}
```

With the preceding code, we told Gatsby to enable the `gatsby-source-drupal` plugin and we have specified the **Uniform Resource Locator** (**URL**) of the Drupal application.

Now that we have installed and configured the plugin, we can start querying our Drupal application through GraphQL.

Querying Drupal with GraphQL

Once the plugin has been configured, we can test it by querying the Drupal application through GraphiQL.

Go to `http://localhost:8000/___graphql` and run the following query:

```
query MyQuery {
  allNodeArticle {
    edges {
      node {
        title
        body {
          value
        }
      }
    }
  }
}
```

This query will return the following result:

```
{
    "data": {
        "allNodeArticle": {
            "edges": [
                {
                    "node": {
                        "title": "Hello world",
                        "body": {
                            "value": "<p>Lean out of the window,<br />\r\
nGoldenhair,<br />\r\nI hear you singing<br />\r\nA merry
air.</p>\r\n\r\n<p>My book was closed,<br />\r\nI read no
more,<br />\r\nWatching the fire dance<br />\r\nOn the floor.</
p>\r\n\r\n<p>I have left my book,<br />\r\nI have left my
room,<br />\r\nFor I heard you singing<br />\r\nThrough the
gloom.</p>\r\n\r\n<p>Singing and singing<br />\r\nA merry
air,<br />\r\nLean out of the window,<br />\r\nGoldenhair.</
p>\r\n"
                        }
                    }
                }
            ]
        }
    }
}
```

In this section, we have installed and configured the gatsby-source-drupal plugin. We have also queried a Drupal application and have retrieved data from the application.

In the next section, we are going to see how we can query both gatsby-source-filesystem and gatsby-source-drupal plugins within one query.

Querying both filesystem and Drupal plugins together

It is possible to query two content sources within the same query, which is advantageous when building a listing page with content coming from different sources.

Our query will contain calls and fields belonging to both plugins. We will get one single response, containing results from both sources separated by their root name. In this case, the Drupal content will be contained under the `allNodeArticle` array, and the filesystem content will be contained under the `AllMarkDownRemark` array.

As we already seen, we can go to `http://localhost:8000/___graphql` and run the following query:

```
query MyQuery {
  allNodeArticle {
    edges {
      node {
        title
        body {
          value
        }
      }
    }
  }
  allMarkdownRemark {
    edges {
      node {
        frontmatter {
          title
          date
          excerpt
        }
        html
      }
    }
  }
}
```

This query will return the following result:

```
{
  "data": {
    "allNodeArticle": {
      "edges": [
        {
          "node": {...}
        }
      ]
    },
    "allMarkdownRemark": {
      "edges": [
        {
          "node": {...}
        }
      ]
    }
  }
}
```

As we can see, we have both the Drupal and filesystem content from the two different sources, in the same query result.

Summary

In this chapter, we learned how to extend Gatsby using plugins to enrich the functionality of the application. We learned about the following: what a plugin is; npm; how to use semantic versioning; and how to install and update a plugin. We also learned about the structure of the Gatsby Plugin Library and how to install and configure a Gatsby plugin. We installed and configured the `gatsby-source-filesystem` and `gatsby-transform-remark` plugins, and we used GraphQL to query content from a Markdown file. We also installed and configured the `gatsby-source-drupal` plugin and used GraphQL to query content from a Drupal application.

These plugins are useful when we need to get content from other sources, especially if we need to build an application that aggregates content from different sources.

In the next chapter, we are going to talk about Gatsby components and how pages, templates, and partials are structured, and how they differ.

Further reading

- Read more regarding semantic versioning at `https://semver.org/`.

- Read more regarding the `gatsby-transformer-remark` plugin at `https://www.gatsbyjs.org/packages/gatsby-transformer-remark/`.

- Read more regarding the `gatsby-source-drupal` plugin at `https://www.gatsbyjs.org/packages/gatsby-source-drupal`.

- Read more regarding the `gatsby-source-filesystem` plugin at `https://www.gatsbyjs.org/packages/gatsby-source-filesystem/`.

10
Building Gatsby Components

This chapter introduces the *M* component of the Jamstack; that is, **Markup**. Markup is most often used to render, or produce, the content that the end user will view in the browser, decorated with some formatting. Code modularity in Gatsby is achieved through the use of components, which are its building blocks. Each component building block that is built using JavaScript and JSX will accept input and return HTML and web content to the browser. In this chapter, we will learn how to create, edit, and extend these components – the building blocks of the site.

Components exist in several forms, so we will also look at how they can produce single pages, exist as page templates, and finally how page partials are structured and how the three differ from one another.

The main topics that we will cover in this chapter are the following:

- React components
- Understanding the types of components

Technical requirements

This chapter requires a terminal program and a source code editor program.

The code files for this chapter can be found at the following link: `https://github.com/PacktPublishing/Jumpstart-Jamstack-Development/tree/chapter_ten`.

React components

Gatsby uses React underneath, so it can take advantage of all that React has to offer. A React component is mostly a JavaScript function that returns something. By leveraging GraphQL, the developer can use Gatsby's source plugin to pass data into the page. Properties are usually sent into the component and then events are passed up. These patterns – props down, events up or data down, and actions up, are used in several JavaScript frameworks and are very easy to understand. Once a React component is created, it may be imported to another component for easy reuse.

Tag convention

As mentioned in the previous section, once a component is created, it can be invoked or used in Gatsby as if it was its own HTML tag, so its use is familiar to those who are familiar with working with HTML tags. This is useful for readability, since the output looks like HTML and not JavaScript code. The convention for working with React components is to encapsulate the name of the component in an HTML tag. It must begin with a capital letter.

To illustrate this concept, for example, if we have a component called *books*, we can include it in our project as follows:

```
<Books />
```

Let's start by looking at the various types of components used in Gatsby.

Understanding the types of components

There are three main types of Gatsby components used in this project: page components, templates, and partial components. Let's look at each type as they all serve a different purpose.

Gatsby page components

One of the simplest types of components used in Gatsby is a page component. Gatsby page components are used only once for single, unique pages, such as the index (home) page, 404 page, or an *about us* page, for example. This page will only be generated once.

Building and modifying Gatsby page components

As mentioned previously, pages are unique. By creating a page component and placing it in the /web/ src/pages folder, Gatsby will automatically generate the page.

The content of a code page in Gatsby can be as simple as the following example, which contains the entire page contents inside a string:

```
// Does not require React because there is no JSX
const AboutUsPage = () => (
   `Who we are: .......`
)
export default AboutUspage
```

The following is a shorter way to write the preceding code:

```
const AboutUsPage = () => {
return `Who we are: .......`
}
```

Enhancing this example by using JSX would allow us to create the following example:

```
//Requires React because this example uses JSX tags.
import React from 'react'

const AboutUsPage = () => (
   <html>
     <body>
     <h1>Who we are:</h1>
       <p>.......</p>
     </body>
   </html>
)
export default AboutUsPage
```

If we were to name the file `about-us.js` and place it in the `/web/src/page/` directory, then running Gatsby would display the following screenshot:

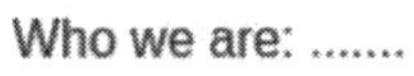

Who we are: ....

Figure 10.1 – Screenshot of the About Us page

This `AboutUsPage` example will be rendered in the browser as HTML.

Gatsby template components

Gatsby template components are, as the name implies, templates. These are used as a template for pages, such as articles, where certain parts of the page will be filled with unique content. These templates will be processed as many times as necessary to produce all the content needed.

Building and modifying template components

To illustrate this concept, we will create a template for the events on our website. The first file that we need to work with is `/web/src/gatsby-node.js`. This file contains the code used to display blog posts using a template.

At the bottom of the `gatsby-node.js` file, the relevant code is as follows:

```
exports.createPages = async ({graphql, actions}) => {
    await createBlogPostPages(graphql, actions)}
```

We will now add another function to generate events sourced from Sanity through GraphQL:

```
exports.createPages = async ({graphql, actions}) => {
    await createBlogPostPages(graphql, actions)
    await createEventPages(graphql, actions)
}
```

Next, we'll copy the content of `createBlogPostPages`. The entire function should be copied. However, the middle of the function was omitted for space. Here is an excerpt:

```
async function createBlogPostPages (graphql, actions) {
    const {createPage} = actions
    const result = await graphql(`
.....
```

```
        createPage({
          path,
          component:
            require.resolve('./src/templates/blog-post.js'),
          context: {id}
        })
      })
  }
```

Here is the structure of the newly created `createEventPages` function:

```
async function createEventPages(graphql, actions) {
  const {createPage} = actions
  const result = await graphql(`
    {
      allSanityEvent {
        ...
      }
    }
  `)
  . . .
  if (result.errors) throw result.errors

  const eventEdges = (result.data.allSanityEvent || {}).edges
|| []
  . . .
  eventEdges
    .forEach((edge, index) => {
      ....
  }
```

Now, let's examine this code. An asynchronous function is created with the `graphql` and `actions` parameters. This will always return a promise:

```
async function createEventPages(graphql, actions) {
```

The `createPage` method is extracted as a constant, or destructured from `actions`:

```
  const {createPage} = actions
```

The constant result is declared to hold the result of the GraphQL query. The JavaScript function will wait for this to complete before moving on. The query is enclosed in backtick operators (`):

```
const result = await graphql(`
    {
```

The following lines are similar to the GraphQL query, which returns Gatsby's id and dataAndTime from allEvents via gatsby-source-sanity:

```
        allSanityEvent {
            edges {
                node {
                    id
                    dateAndTime
                }
            }
        }
    }
`)
```

If there are any errors, throw an exception:

```
    if (result.errors) throw result.errors
```

Next, we'll examine the following line of code:

```
    const eventEdges = (result.data.allSanityEvent || {}).edges
|| []
```

Declare a constant named eventEdges and assign the results of the query's edges to it if they are not empty. Otherwise, if there are no results, then instantiate an empty array to eventEdges. Remember that the result of the GraphQL query is wrapped in data.

Iterate, or loop through (using forEach) all of the edges, using an edge variable for each single edge of the GraphQL query:

```
    eventEdges
        .forEach((edge, index) => {
```

Destructure `id` and `dateAndTime` from the edge's node object:

```
const {id, dateAndTime} = edge.node
```

Use the `format` function from `date-fns`, which is included in the Gatsby `package.json` file to format `dateAndTime`, which otherwise would print as `2020-04-10T15:30:00.000Z`, into a more acceptable four-digit year, front slash, double-digit numeric month format, (YYYY/MM), assigning it to a constant named `dateSegment`:

```
const {format} = require('date-fns')
const dateSegment = format(dateAndTime, 'YYYY/MM')
```

Create the path that will actually be the single page's URL and be seen in the browser. Here, we are using Gatsby's ID, which is created, and not Sanity's ID, which can be accessed in the GraphQL query as `_id`:

```
const path = `/event/${dateSegment}/${id}/`
```

Here is an example of the URL path:

```
/event/2021/09/dd88fc6c-10c5-572e-8c58-696add54a14a/
```

Finally, the `createPage` function is called, passing in the path, specifying the `event.js` template file for each page, and passing in `id` as the `context` parameter:

```
createPage({
    path,
    component:
        require.resolve('./src/templates/event.js'),
    context: {id}
  })
})
}
```

The contents of the `event.js` file will be used in the `component` attribute of the `createPage` method and will be resolved, combining the contents of the page and its template to produce a single page.

Building the event.js template

event.js is the template used for each individual event page, so let's look at how it is constructed:

1. First, we need a few import statements to bring in the necessary features:

```
import React from 'react'
import {graphql} from 'gatsby'
import Container from '../components/container'
import GraphQLErrorList from '../components/graphql-error-list'
import Event from '../components/event'
import SEO from '../components/seo'
import Layout from '../containers/layout'
import {toPlainText} from '../lib/helpers'
```

2. Next, we need to perform a GraphQL query to obtain each element of the page:

```
export const query = graphql`
  query EventTemplateQuery($id: String!) {
    event: sanityEvent(id: {eq: $id}) {
      name
      _rawBody
      venue {
        name
      }
    }
  }
`
```

At a minimum, to produce the event's page, we need its name, _rawBody, and the name of the event's related venue.

3. Next, `EventTemplate` is defined with `props` (properties) as its parameter and eventually exported:

```
const EventTemplate = props => {
    ...
}

export default EventTemplate
```

4. Next, the `data` and `errors` (if present) objects are deconstructed from the `props` parameter. Then, if `data` is present, the event constant is instantiated to hold the data object's `event`:

```
const {data, errors} = props
const event = data && data.event
```

5. Next, the `Layout` component is called inside the `SEO` component and the `Event` component. The error handling code has been removed to remove any distraction, but errors would be displayed here as well if they existed. The layout produces the page layout, tags, such as the header and footer, and provides a wrapper for the event:

```
return (
    <Layout>
        {event && <SEO title={event.name || 'Untitled'} />}

        {event && <Event {...event} />}
    </Layout>
)
```

> **Note**
>
> Notice how the JavaScript ES6 spread syntax is used to assign each of the `Event` object's values to separate values to be used with the `Event` component.

This `Event` tag represents an example of components that can be easily inserted into numerous contexts. In the following *Figure 10.2*, we see how an example event will be displayed on the page:

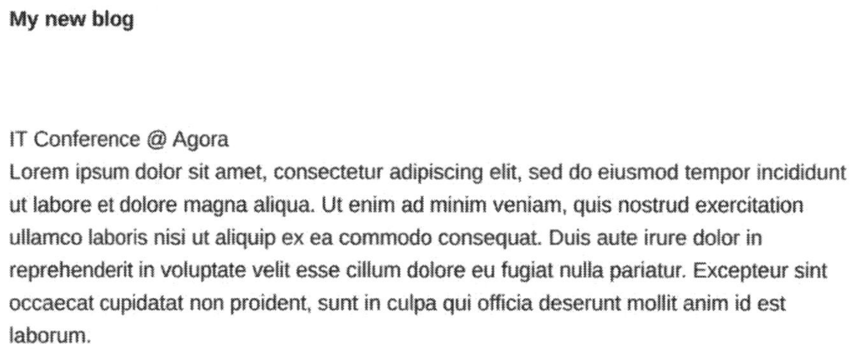

My new blog

IT Conference @ Agora

Lorem ipsum dolor sit amet, consectetur adipiscing elit, sed do eiusmod tempor incididunt ut labore et dolore magna aliqua. Ut enim ad minim veniam, quis nostrud exercitation ullamco laboris nisi ut aliquip ex ea commodo consequat. Duis aute irure dolor in reprehenderit in voluptate velit esse cillum dolore eu fugiat nulla pariatur. Excepteur sint occaecat cupidatat non proident, sunt in culpa qui officia deserunt mollit anim id est laborum.

Figure 10.2 – An event

In the next section, we'll look at how an example in-page or partial component is constructed.

Gatsby partial components

Partials, as some frontend systems refer to them, are non-page components, such as a header or an element of a page that can be embedded and reused many times throughout the website.

Building and modifying Gatsby partial components

Gatsby partials have a format similar to other components. However, there are several differences. The main difference is that they are not complete pages, so they cannot be rendered as such. Also, they will be embedded in files by importing them.

Let's look at how a partial component file is constructed:

1. First, a few `import` statements bring in a few libraries for added functionality and auxiliary:

```
import React from 'react'
import {buildImageObj} from '../lib/helpers'
import {imageUrlFor} from '../lib/image-url'
import PortableText from './portableText'
import Container from './container'
```

2. To start, we will continue to use the cascading style sheet from the blog post:

```
import styles from './blog-post.module.css'
```

3. Next, the Event function is defined and the properties of the single event are passed into the function through the props parameter. The function is exported at the end:

```
:
function Event (props) {
...
}
export default Event
```

The _rawBody, name, and venue objects are destructured from the props parameter as they are necessary for the page contents:

```
const {_rawBody, name, venue} = props
```

4. Finally, the contents of the page are produced and returned:

```
return (
...
)
```

5. An article tag is a standard semantic in HTML5 and here is used as the outermost tag, enclosing the contents:

```
<article className={styles.root}>

    <Container>
        <div className={styles.grid}>
            <div className={styles.mainContent}>
```

6. Here, we print the name of the event and the venue name, using dot notation, since the venue name is contained within the venue object. Note that the dynamic elements are enclosed in curly braces so as to be replaced with the actual values:

```
            <h1 className={styles.name}>{name} @ {venue.name}
    </h1>
```

7. Finally, a trick is employed here to instruct Gatsby to display _rawBody if it exists using a logical *and*. The double ampersand is used to denote *and*. The format is *if a and b*. Here, if *a* is *false*, meaning that _rawBody has no contents, then the `<PortableText>` tag and its contents, _rawBody, will not be displayed.

PortableText is a component that converts Sanity's content, _rawBody, to React content so that it can be displayed properly:

```
                    {_rawBody && <PortableText blocks={_rawBody}
    />}
            </div>
        </div>
          </Container>
        </article>
```

The following diagram is an example of how the page will be displayed:

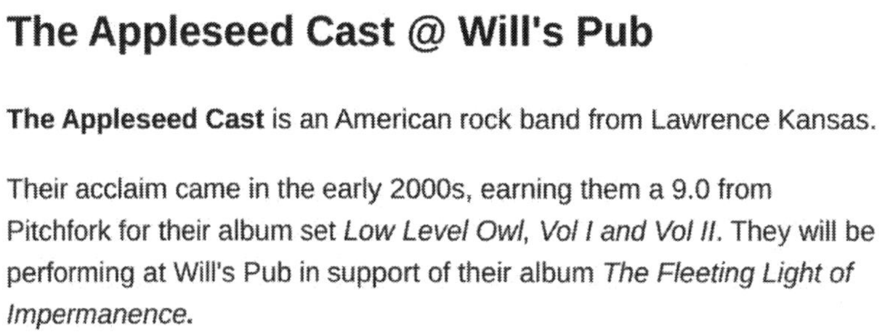

The Appleseed Cast @ Will's Pub

The Appleseed Cast is an American rock band from Lawrence Kansas.

Their acclaim came in the early 2000s, earning them a 9.0 from Pitchfork for their album set *Low Level Owl, Vol I and Vol II*. They will be performing at Will's Pub in support of their album *The Fleeting Light of Impermanence.*

Figure 10.3 – An example Gatsby page

Summary

In this chapter, we learned about page, template, and partial components. The page component represents a unique page, a template is used to produce many similar types of pages, and partials are pieces of content that can be used within other pages. Each type of component used in Gatsby is based on React, so it reutilizes a robust JavaScript-based system. These components are the building blocks of Gatsby, so knowing how to create and work with them is essential to all Gatsby development.

In the next chapter, we will begin our journey into the *A* part of the Jamstack acronym – the API.

11

APIs – Extending Gatsby

In this chapter, you will learn about the *A* part of the Jamstack—that is, **Application Programming Interfaces** (**APIs**). We will learn how to use them within the dynamic portion of a compiled web page to recreate the functionality that web developers are familiar with in traditional server-based web development. We are going to create a custom **Propose an event** form using a Netlify form, and we are going to manage submissions through Netlify functions. We will also see how to connect a third-party service to our Gatsby application.

We will cover the following topics in this chapter:

- Introduction to APIs
- Gatsby – APIs

Technical requirements

We will need the following applications to thoroughly understand this chapter:

- Terminal
- The Gatsby application installed
- A Netlify account

The code files for this chapter can be found at `https://github.com/PacktPublishing/Jumpstart-Jamstack-Development/tree/chapter_eleven`.

Introduction to APIs

APIs have been around almost since we started programming. Modern APIs started to become as we know them now in the early 2000s, when companies such as Amazon started to provide access to their data through **HyperText Transfer Protocol** (**HTTP**) requests. These companies changed the way we did business online. Developers could now get and post user information from services such as Salesforce and provide a full e-commerce experience on their application using APIs.

In 2004, with the introduction of social networks, we changed the way we were using the internet. Companies such as Facebook and Twitter started developing their own APIs. Similar to the e-commerce experience, developers could now get a user's profile information, events, and pictures from social networking applications.

A few years later, the new generation of smartphones came out. People started navigating the internet through their mobile phones and developers started developing applications that could be installed on a smartphone, and APIs were the right way to connect to these services. Instagram changed the way we were sharing photos on the internet and provided their own API a few years later.

Around 2010, we had desktop and smartphone devices consuming APIs and relying on third-party web services through web applications and mobile applications and, around 2015, more devices got *smarter*. Every device that could connect to the internet could access the API resources of a web service. Smart speakers, thermostats, watches, and many other devices started consuming APIs.

Amazon Alexa, Google Nest, Fitbit, and Apple Watch are just a few of many devices we now use every day that can get data from APIs.

Let's explore the Gatsby API in the next section.

Gatsby – APIs

In this section, we are going to explore how to use APIs inside Gatsby. In the example that we will build in this chapter, we will create an event form whereby anonymous users can propose their event. When the user submits the form, we will add the submission to Sanity via an API.

To achieve this, we will do the following:

- Create a Netlify form on the home page of our events application.
- Configure a token from Sanity so that we can submit the form via an API.
- Configure a Netlify function to send data on submission.

Creating a Netlify form

As our third-party service, we will use Netlify Forms, a built-in form-handling functionality provided by Netlify. When the code is deployed to Netlify, the system automatically detects the form and creates a form submission page in your Netlify site's admin panel.

To create a Netlify form, simply add the `netlify="true"` attribute data to the `<form>` tag, add the `<input type="hidden" name="form-name" value="YOUR_VALUE" />` hidden field, and you are ready to go.

Our form will have the following fields:

- **Full Name**
- **Email**
- **Event title**
- **Date**
- **Venue**
- **Virtual**
- **Event URL**
- **Description**

We will add our form to our home page just before the footer, as follows:

1. Open the `index.js` file located under `/web/src/pages/`.
2. Right before the closing container tag (`</Container>`) we can add our form, like this:

```
<form name="propose-event" method="POST" data-
netlify="true" >
  <input type="hidden" name="form-name" value="propose-
event" />
</form>
```

As you can see, we have added the two parameters needed to be able to submit a form into Netlify.

3. Let's keep adding the other fields, as follows:

```
<form name='propose-event' method='POST' data-
netlify='true'  >
        <input type='hidden' name='form-name'
value='propose-event' />
        <div className='field'>
          <label className='label'>Full name:
            <input className='input' type='text'
name='name'/>
          </label>
        </div>
        <div className='field'>
          <label className='label'>Email:
            <input className='input' type='email'
name='email'/>
          </label>
        </div>
        ...
        <div className='field'>
          <label className='label'>Message:
            <textarea className='textarea'
name='message'></textarea>
          </label>
        </div>
        <div className='field'>
          <button className='button' type='submit'>Send
          </button>
        </div>
      </form>
```

The venue field will get venues from our site. Let's add the query to get all the venues.

4. In our `index.js` page, inside the `IndexPageQuery` query, we can add the query to get all the IDs and names of the venues, as follows:

```
Query IndexPageQuery {
    ...
    venues: allSanityVenue {
        edges {
            node {
                _id
                name
            }
        }
    }
    ...
```

5. Map the data inside a constant called `venueNodes`, as illustrated in the following code snippet:

```
const venueNodes = (data || {}).venues
    ? mapEdgesToNodes(data.venues)
    : []
```

6. Add our `venue` field to the form, like this:

```
<div className="field">
    <label className="label">Venue:
        <select className="select" name="venue">
            {
                venueNodes && venueNodes.map((venue) => (
                    <option id={venue._id}>{venue.name}</option>
                ))
            }
        </select>
    </label>
</div>
```

Now that our HTML form is ready, it should look like this:

Figure 11.1 – Form under the Gatsby application home page

We are ready to push it to GitHub.

Deploying the form to Netlify

As we know, when we push the code up GitHub, it automatically deploys to Netlify as shown in the following steps:

1. Once it is deployed to Netlify, we will be able to see the form in our Netlify site's admin panel under the **Forms** tab, as illustrated in the following screenshot:

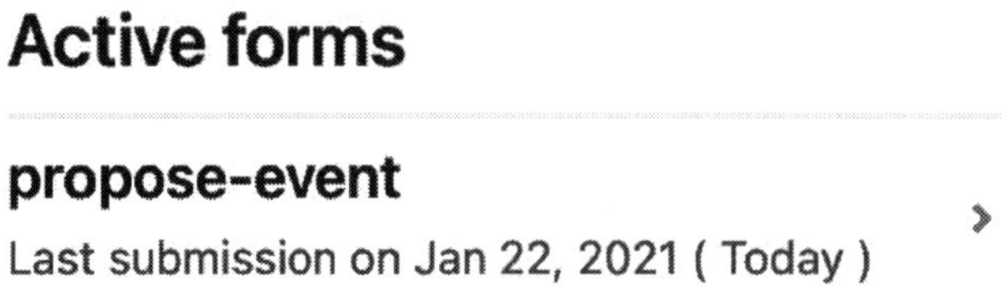

Active forms

propose-event

Last submission on Jan 22, 2021 (Today)   >

Figure 11.2 – Forms tab

2. If you click on **Forms**, you will see **Submissions**, as depicted in the following screenshot:

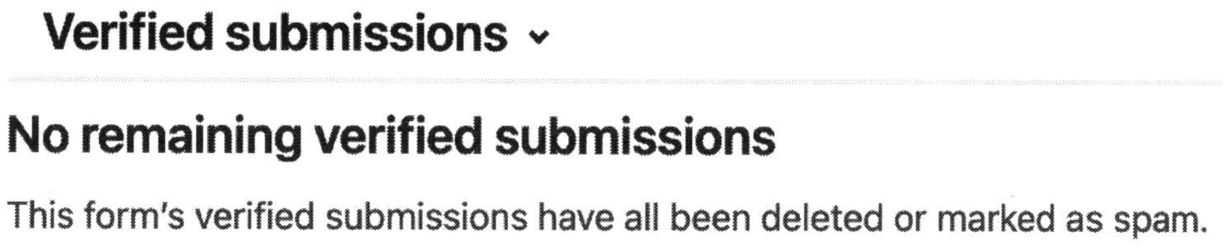

Verified submissions ⌄

No remaining verified submissions

This form's verified submissions have all been deleted or marked as spam.

Figure 11.3 – Netlify Forms page

Let's add a new submission.

3. Go to your Gatsby live site on Netlify and complete the form. After you click **Send**, you will receive the following confirmation message:

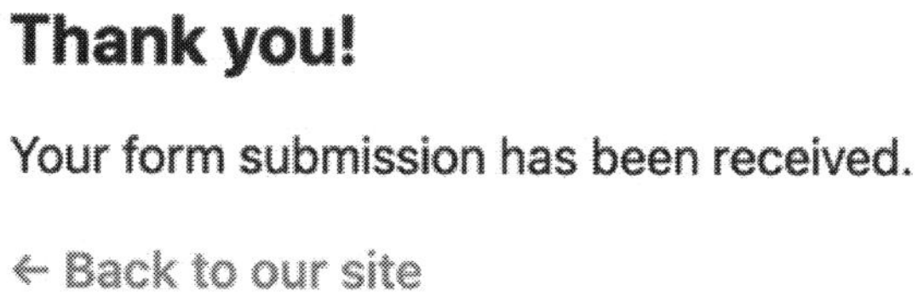

Thank you!

Your form submission has been received.

← Back to our site

Figure 11.4 – Netlify submission success page

4. Now, let's go back to the Netlify form admin panel to see our submission, as illustrated in the following screenshot:

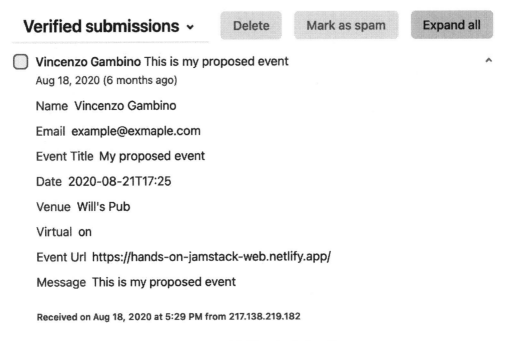

Figure 11.5 – Netlify submissions list

As you can see, we have our form submission on Netlify.

Now, let's extend our form and use the Sanity API to get and insert information.

Configuring a token form in Sanity

When a new form is submitted, we need to add a new event into our Sanity application. In order to do that, we create a token that gives permission to our function to access Sanity and create an `Event`.

We also need to add a new `'approved'` field to our events so that we avoid the publication of unwanted events on our Sanity application.

Creating an approved field

We will create a `boolean` field that will define whether an event has been approved or not.

Open the event schema file located under `studio/schemas/documents.index.js` and add the new field inside the `fields` array, like this:

```
export default {
  name: 'event',
  type: 'document',
  title: 'Event',
  fields: [
    ...
    {
      name: 'approved',
      type: 'boolean',
      title: 'Approved'
    },
    ...
  ]
}
```

Save the file and restart your local application. Now, you should see the field in your local Sanity application.

To deploy the field to production, from the Terminal go inside the `/studio` folder and type the following command:

```
sanity graphql deploy
```

Deploying a Sanity token

As a first step, we will generate a new token specifically for this form. To do that, go into your **Manage Sanity** admin panel (`https://manage.sanity.io/`) and click on your project. Then, proceed as follows:

1. Go to **Site Settings | API** and scroll down to **Tokens**. The existing token is used by Gatsby to retrieve the content from Sanity. Now, we need to generate a new token to write data into Sanity.

2. Click on the blue **ADD NEW TOKEN** button, as illustrated in the following screenshot:

Figure 11.6 – Tokens

3. Insert a title, and then select the **Rights** permission as **Write**. This permission gives the user the ability (right) to read, write, and delete data. Now, click on the green **ADD NEW TOKEN** button, as illustrated in the following screenshot:

Label

To create a new token, please provide a label for it. Examples: "Employee import", "Website preview" or "PDF generator"

ProposedEvents

Rights

○ Read   ⦿ Write   ○ Deploy studio

Can read, write and delete data.

Figure 11.7 – Adding a new token

A new token is generated and prompted to you.

4. Copy the token, and now go back to your Netlify project and click on **Settings | Build & deploy | Environment**.

    In this section of the settings, it is possible to store the token securely as an environment variable, as highlighted in the following screenshot:

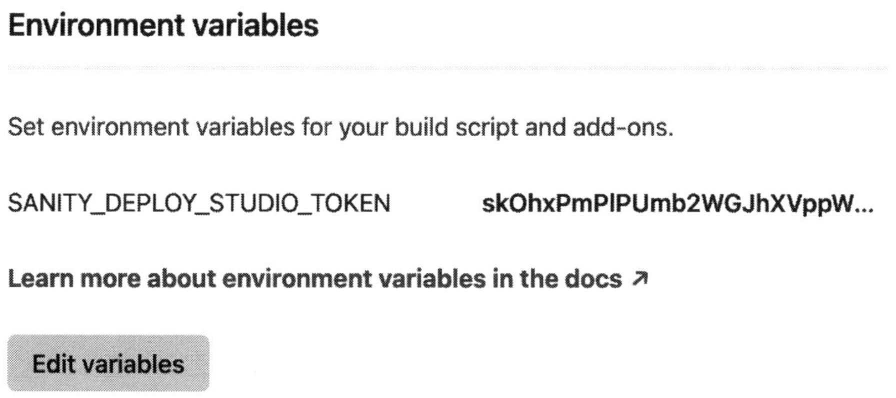

Environment variables

Set environment variables for your build script and add-ons.

SANITY_DEPLOY_STUDIO_TOKEN   **skOhxPmPlPUmb2WGJhXVppW...**

Learn more about environment variables in the docs ↗

Edit variables

Figure 11.8 – Netlify Environment variables settings page

5. Click on **Edit variables | New variable**.

6. Add your new token, called SANITY_STUDIO_PROPOSE_EVENT, and click on **Save**, as illustrated in the following screenshot:

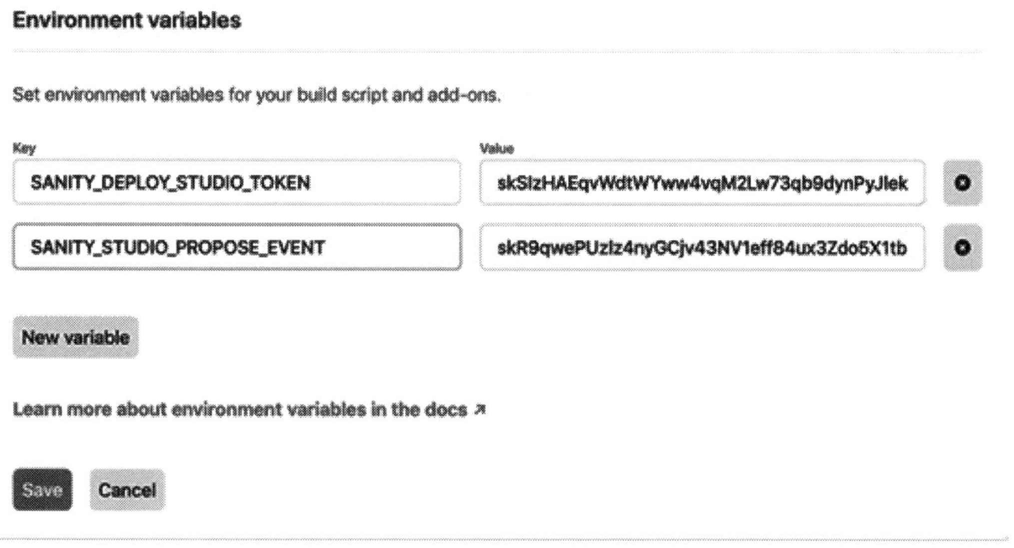

Environment variables

Set environment variables for your build script and add-ons.

Key	Value	
SANITY_DEPLOY_STUDIO_TOKEN	skSIzHAEqvWdtWYww4vqM2Lw73qb9dynPyJlek	⊗
SANITY_STUDIO_PROPOSE_EVENT	skR9qwePUzlz4nyGCjv43NV1eff84ux3Zdo5X1tb	⊗

New variable

Learn more about environment variables in the docs ↗

Save   Cancel

Figure 11.9 – Netlify Environment variables settings page

Now that we have the token in place, we can insert a new document into Sanity with our custom form.

Configuring a Netlify function

Netlify functions are **Amazon Web Services (AWS)** Lambda functions that let you run code without configuring or managing servers.

Let's see how to configure it inside Netlify, as follows:

1. As a first step, we need to tell Netlify in which directory our serverless functions are. Netlify will look into the given directory on each deployment, and it will deploy the functions into AWS.

2. Let's create a folder named functions inside our web directory, and a Netlify configuration file called netlify.toml.

   Inside our netlify.toml file we can tell where our functions will be, as illustrated in the following code snippet:

   ```
   [build]
      base = "."
      functions = "./web/functions"
   ```

3. As a first test, we will create a simple *Hello World* script.

4. Create a hello-world.js file inside web/functions and add the following code:

   ```
   // /web/functions/hello-world.js
   exports.handler = async function() {
     return {
       statusCode: 200,
       body: "Hello world from a Netlify Function!",
     };
   }
   ```

   Great—we have now created our first function. The function will be available under https://yoursite.com/.netlify/functions/hello-world.

5. To run it locally, we need to install the Netlify command-line tool. To do that, from the Terminal type the following command:

   ```
   npm install -g netlify-cli
   ```

6. Once the `netlify-cli` tool is installed, from the Terminal go into the /web directory and type the following command:

```
netlify link
```

7. Select the correct project by selecting the project created in GitHub when prompted by the following message:

```
Vincenzos-MacBook-Pro:hands-on-jamstack vincenzogambino$ netlify link

netlify link will connect this folder to a site on Netlify

? How do you want to link this folder to a site? (Use arrow keys)
> Use current git remote origin (https://github.com/VincenzoGambino/hands-on-jamstack)
  Search by full or partial site name
  Choose from a list of your recently updated sites
  Enter a site ID
```

Figure 11.10 – Terminal

8. Select the Gatsby application (the one that ends with `web`); that is `hands-on-jamstack-web` in our case, as illustrated in the following screenshot:

```
Looking for sites connected to 'https://github.com/VincenzoGambino/hands-on-jamstack'...

Found 2 matching sites!
? Which site do you want to link? (Use arrow keys)
> hands-on-jamstack-web - https://hands-on-jamstack-web.netlify.app
  hands-on-jamstack-studio - https://hands-on-jamstack-studio.netlify.app
```

Figure 11.11 – Terminal

Now, the linking is done.

9. Once the link is done, inside the web directory type the following command:

```
netlify dev
```

This command will start your Gatsby project and set up an AWS Lambda server, and it launches a server on port `8888`.

10. Now, you can access your local site from `http://localhost:8888` and see your function output from `http://localhost:8888/.netlify/functions/hello-world`, as illustrated in the following screenshot:

Hello world from a Netlify Function!

Figure 11.12 – Netlify function on our Gatsby application

In this section, we have created a new Netlify form on our Gatsby home page, created a token on Sanity to let Netlify insert a new proposed event, and configured our Netlify function folder.

In the next section, we are going to create a function that inserts a new proposed event into our Sanity dataset.

Creating the submission-created.js file

Netlify form submission triggers a `submission-created` event. Execute the following steps to create the `.js` file:

1. Create a file inside `web/functions` called `submission-created.js`. This function will handle submissions from the Netlify form.

2. Next, create `export.handler` for this function, as follows:

```
exports.handler = async (event, context, callback) => {
}
```

This handler receives an event object that contains `path`, `httpMethod`, `headers`, `queryStrinparameters`, `body`, and `isBase64Encoded`.

The `context` parameter includes information such as user identity information. The `callback` parameter is similar to the `callback` parameter in an AWS Lambda function. The code can be seen in the following snippet:

```
exports.handler = function(event, context, callback) {
    callback(null, {
    statusCode: 200,
    body: "Hello, World"
    });
}
```

Sanity provides the Client API to add content via the API.

3. In our `submission-created.js` file, let's add the client at the top of the file, like this:

```
const sanityClient = require('@sanity/client')
exports.handler = function(event, context, callback) {
    callback(null, {
    statusCode: 200,
    body: "Hello, World"
    });
}
```

4. To initialize the client, we need to provide the Sanity project ID, dataset name, and an access token. In our Sanity application home page, our local is under `http://localhost:3333`. Get the project ID and the dataset used from your Sanity manager console.

5. We have created the access token in the previous section, and we can now reuse it, as follows:

```
const sanityClient = require('@sanity/client')
const client = sanityClient({
   projectId: 'my_project_id',
   dataset: 'my_dataset',
   token: process.env.SANITY_STUDIO_ADD_EVENT
})
exports.handler = function(event, context, callback) {
    callback(null, {
    statusCode: 200,
    body: "Hello, World"
    });
}
```

6. Now, we can use the `create(doc)` method to add a new event to Sanity.

7. The `client` method requires a plain JavaScript object representing the document. It must include a `_type` attribute.

Let's start building our document. Our `Events` fields are as follows:

```
Title
Date
Event URL
Venue
Virtual
Description
```

8. Inside our `handler`, we must get the `body` of the event, as follows:

```
exports.handler = async function(event, context,
callback) {
  const { payload } = JSON.parse(event.body)
  ...
}
```

9. Now, we can map the fields inside the payload, like this:

```
const doc = {
  _type: 'event',
  name: payload.data.eventTitle,
  dateAndTime: payload.data.date,
  virtual: payload.data.virtual === 'on',
  eventUrl: payload.data.eventUrl,
  venue: {
    _ref: payload.data.venue,
    _type: 'reference'
  },
  body: [{
    '_type': 'block',
    'children': [{
      '_type': 'span',
      'text': payload.data.message
    }]
  }],
  approved: false
}
```

10. Now that our document is ready, we can pass it to the `create(doc)` function, as follows:

```
const sanityClient = require('@sanity/client')
const client = sanityClient({
  projectId: 'my_project_id',
  dataset: 'my_dataset',
  token: process.env.SANITY_STUDIO_ADD_EVENT
})
exports.handler = async function(event, context,
callback) {
  const { payload } = JSON.parse(event.body)
  const doc = {
    ...
  }


  // Create document
  await client.create(doc)
    .then(res => {
      callback(null, {statusCode: 200})
    })
}
```

And it's done. Now, add the code to Git and push it to the master. Once the deployment is finished, we can test it in our production environment.

In your live Gatsby application, fill in the form and press **Send**, as shown in *Figure 11.1*. A new submission will be added on Netlify Forms, and the content will be added to Sanity from Gatsby using the Netlify function.

Summary

In this chapter, we have learned how to use Netlify Forms to help make creating and managing form submissions frictionless. We have extended the Netlify form with our own action on submit, using the power of the Netlify functions. At the end, we used the Sanity API to create new `Event` content from a Netlify form using Netlify functions.

In the next chapter, we are going to create an Alexa skill that will read events from our Sanity dataset.

12
APIs – Alexa Skills

Alexa is the Amazon Virtual Assistant that can perform tasks or services for an individual, and it uses natural language processing and machine learning to convert voice input to an executable command. Alexa can provide a wide variety of services, from music playback to creating to-do lists, playing audiobooks, and providing weather, traffic, and news. Alexa is also capable of controlling many smart devices, allowing you to build an automation system for your home. An Amazon user can install skills, which are functionalities, similar to apps, that are available in the Alexa Skills Store to extend Alexa's capabilities.

In this chapter, we will build the Jumpstart Jamstack Alexa skill. A user would be able to ask for the upcoming five events. Through this example, you will be able to extend the current skill by retrieving past events, or all events, and you will also be able to create a new skill for any other application you have.

We will cover the following topics in this chapter:

- Alexa skill life cycle
- Creating the skill

Technical requirements

To develop an Alexa skill, you must have access to the Alexa Developer Console by creating an account at `https://developer.amazon.com/alexa`. In addition to this, you need Sanity Studio installed on your system.

The code for this chapter is available at `https://github.com/PacktPublishing/Jumpstart-Jamstack-Development/tree/chapter_twelve`.

Alexa skill life cycle

A user activates a particular skill by saying the trigger word *Alexa* followed by the skill name and the intent (command) to be executed. For example, *Alexa, ask jumpstart jamstack to tell me my upcoming events.*

The Amazon Echo device will send the request to the Alexa console, which will then process the request by contacting our Sanity application and will send the results back to the Amazon Echo device, prompting a message to the user.

To build an Alexa skill, we will use the Alexa Developer console. The two components of an Alexa skill are the skill interface and the skill service.

Skill interface

The **Skill interface** is the software provided by Amazon where the user can develop an Alexa skill through a nice and clean UI. We will use the skill interface to create and modify each component of the skill.

Skill service

The **Skill service** is where the business logic of an Alexa skill resides. The code will execute the intent and return a JSON response to the interface that will give the user an understandable human sentence as a response.

In this chapter, our service will be executed in Node.js inside an AWS Lambda function.

Now that we know what the skill interface and skill service are, we will move on to creating the skill for Alexa.

Creating the skill

As mentioned earlier, we are going to create a skill through the **Alexa Developer Console**, which will retrieve five upcoming events from our event website.

From the interface, we will create a new intent with a simple utterance:

1. Log in to the Amazon Developer Console and click on the **Alexa** link as shown:

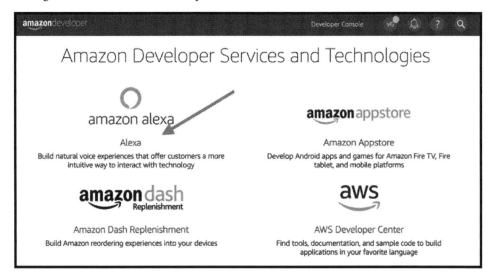

Figure 12.1 – Amazon Developer Console

2. Now, from the top menu, click on the **Skill Builders** link and then the **Developer Console** link, as shown:

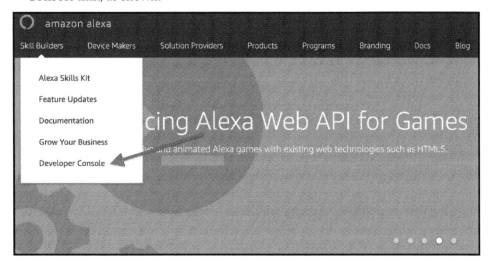

Figure 12.2 – Amazon Alexa console

The Alexa Developer Console will show all the skills you have created, along with revenue that you are earning through **Skills**, **Earnings**, **Payments**, and **Hosting**.

3.   Click on the blue button that says **Create Skill**:

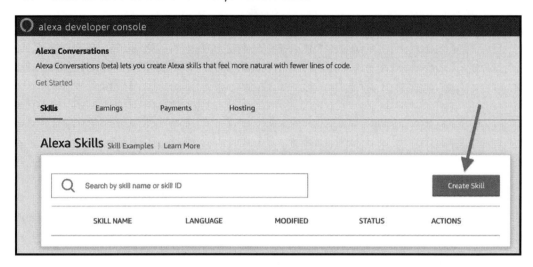

Figure 12.3 – Amazon Alexa Skills overview

4.   Choose a skill name that will also be your invocation name. For this example, we will write `jumpstart jamstack`:

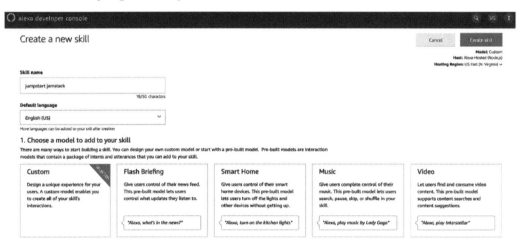

Figure 12.4 – Amazon Alexa Skills creation page

Models in the Alexa paradigm are sets of intents and utterances that define the usage of your skill. In this example, we will use the **Custom** model.

5. As mentioned previously, we will use the Alexa-hosted host, so use the default selected **Alexa-Hosted (Node.js)**:

Figure 12.5 – Amazon Alexa Skills creation page

In the top-right corner, if you want, you can change the region where the skill is hosted. I left it as the default **US East (N. Virginia)**.

6. Then, click on the **Create skill** blue button in the top-right corner to create the skill:

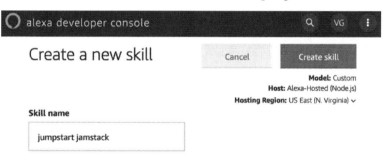

Figure 12.6 – Amazon Alexa Skills creation page

7. Choose the default selected **Hello World Skill** template and click on the blue button in the top-right corner labeled **Continue with template**:

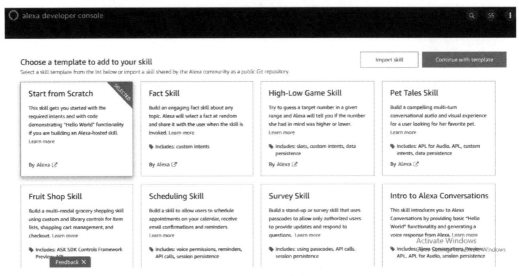

Figure 12.7 – Amazon Alexa Skills creation page

Now that we have created a new Alexa skill, we are ready to configure it through the skill interface.

Configuring the skill through the skill interface

Once the skill has been created, we land on our skill interface. In the top menu, we have the following six options, as shown in the screenshot:

- **Build**
- **Code**
- **Test**
- **Distribution**
- **Certification**
- **Analytics**

Figure 12.8 – Alexa skill interface top menu

Since this is an example skill, we will be exploring **Build**, **Code**, and **Test** in this chapter. The **Distribution**, **Certification**, and **Analytics** tabs are used when the skill is added to the marketplace.

Build

The **Build** section is where we can set the invocation name, configure the interaction model, set slots, and set the endpoint:

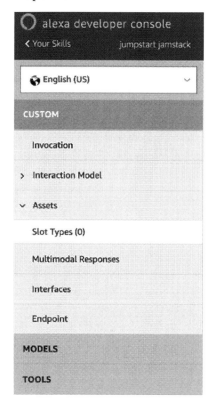

Figure 12.9 – Alexa skill interface build menu

Invocation

The invocation name is the keyword we need to interact with our skill. Our invocation name is `jumpstart jamstack`, so we can say *Alexa, open jumpstart jamstack*:

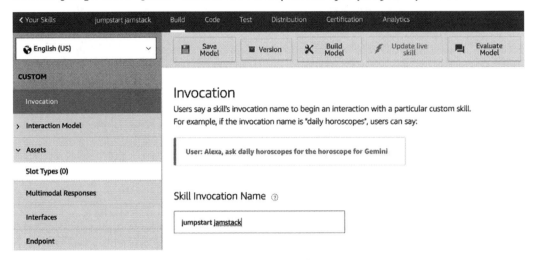

Figure 12.10 – Alexa skill interface: Invocation tab

Interaction model

In the interaction model, we can set out intents and utterances. The following four default built-in intents are created with any Alexa skill:

- `CancelIntent`
- `HelpIntent`
- `StopIntent`
- `NavigateHomeIntent`

`CancelIntent` and `StopIntent` are similar and are called when you want to stop an interaction. For example, when Alexa is reading a set of news for you, you can say, *Alexa stop* and Alexa will stop reading the news, or while you are listening to music through Alexa, `StopIntent` and `CancelIntent` are called when you want to stop the playback.

`HelpIntent` is used when you would like to know more about a skill and what utterances are available.

`NavigateHomeIntent` is used when you are using a multi-level skill and you would like to go back to the top menu of the skill.

In our list of intent, we also have our default `HelloWorldIntent`, which contains seven utterances. Let's now add `GetUpcomingEventsIntent`:

1.   Click on the **Add Intent** blue button above the intent list:

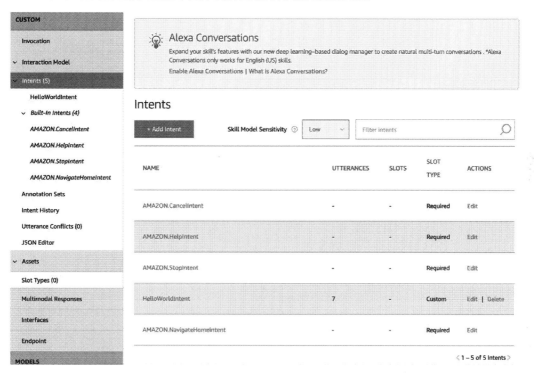

Figure 12.11 – Alexa skill interface Intents tab

2. In our **Create custom intent** section, add the name of the intent as
    GetUpcomingEventsIntent. Then, click the blue **Create custom intent** button:

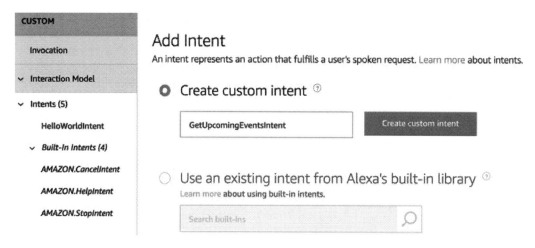

Figure 12.12 – Alexa skill interface Add Intent page

Amazon also provides a set of intents that can be used for certain skills such as weather, video, and audio.

Now that we have created our custom intent, we can start adding our utterances.

A user may ask, *Alexa, ask jumpstart jamstack for the upcoming events*, or *Alexa, ask jumpstart jamstack to tell me the upcoming events.*

We can add as many utterances as we would like. For this example, let's add the following utterances:

- list me the upcoming events
- tell me the upcoming events
- what are the upcoming events

To add an utterance, execute the following steps:

1. Write it in the **Sample Utterances** textbox and then press the + button on the right of the textbox. If you don't click on the + button, the utterance will not be added:

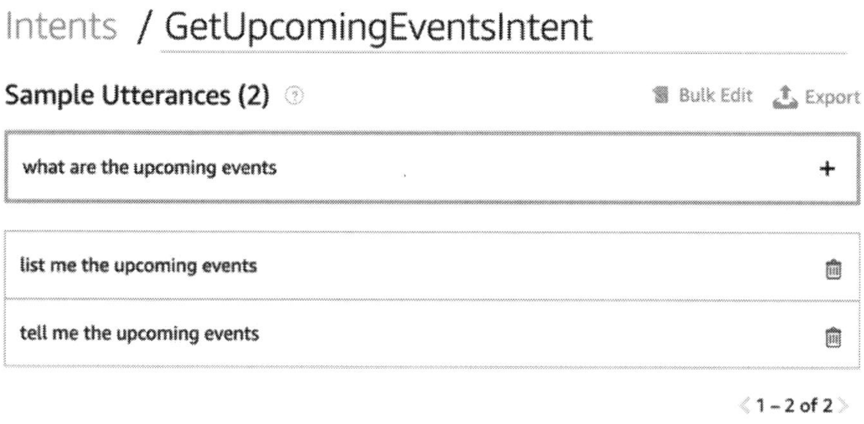

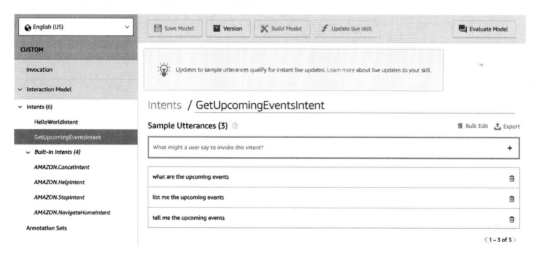

Figure 12.13 – Alexa skill interface Intents page

Now you should have three utterances added to your intent.

2. Click on the **Save Model** button above the **Intents** form and then click on **Build Model** beside the **Save Model** button:

Figure 12.14 – Alexa skill interface Intents page

Now our Intent has been added and the model has been built and is ready to be used in our Alexa service.

In this section, we have created a new intent to retrieve our events and we have rebuilt the model to activate the new intent. In the next section, we will check the intent history.

Intent history

Clicking on the **Intent History** link on the left-hand side menu, you can check all the frequent intent requests done to your skill in the last 30 days. You can check **Unresolved Utterances** and **Resolved Utterances**. From here, you can improve your intent utterances:

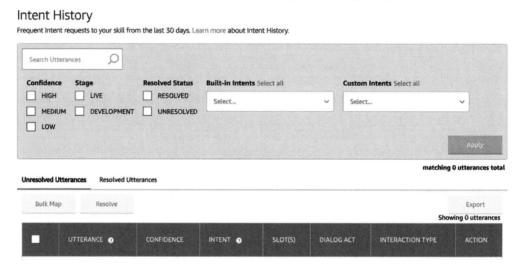

Figure 12.15 – Alexa skill Intent History page

Utterance conflicts

Clicking on **Utterance Conflicts** on the left-hand side menu, you can see whether there are conflicting utterances between intentions:

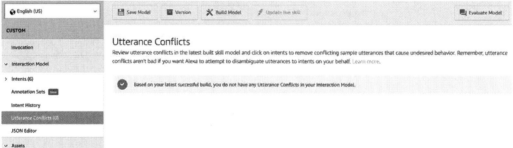

Figure 12.16 – Alexa skill Utterance Conflicts page

JSON Editor

Clicking on **JSON Editor** on the left-hand side menu, you can also create intents via JSON code. This is useful when you want to import an existing intent quickly from another skill:

JSON Editor

Click here to learn more about the schema definition for interaction models.

Drag and drop a .json file

```
1  {
2      "interactionModel": {
3          "languageModel": {
4              "invocationName": "jumpstart jamstack",
5              "intents": [
6                  {
7                      "name": "AMAZON.CancelIntent",
8                      "samples": []
9                  },
10                 {
11                     "name": "AMAZON.HelpIntent",
12                     "samples": []
13                 },
14                 {
15                     "name": "AMAZON.StopIntent",
16                     "samples": []
17                 },
18                 {
19                     "name": "HelloWorldIntent",
20                     "slots": [],
21                     "samples": [
22                         "hello",
23                         "how are you",
24                         "say hi world",
25                         "say hi",
26                         "hi",
27                         "say hello world",
28                         "say hello"
29                     ]
30                 },
31                 {
32                     "name": "AMAZON.NavigateHomeIntent",
33                     "samples": []
34                 }
35             ],
36             "types": []
37         }
38     }
39  }
```

Figure 12.17 – Alexa Skill JSON Editor page

Slot types

Slots can see a variable passed via an utterance. By default, Amazon provides many slot types, such as number, city, and country, that are recognized by Alexa. You can also create a custom slot type and process it at your convenience.

An example of a slot type can be found in a weather skill when you enquire about the weather in a particular city.

In your `WeatherByCity` intents, you don't need to add an utterance for each city in the world, and you can pass it as a variable:

Figure 12.18 – Alexa skill Slot Types page

Endpoint

Endpoint will receive the JSON payload request. We can leave the default here as we are using an AWS Lambda function.

If you want to host your Alexa service somewhere other than AWS, you can select the **HTTPS** option:

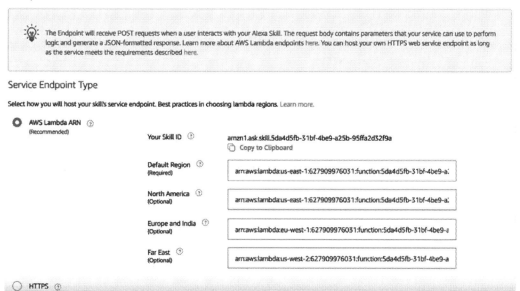

Figure 12.19 – Alexa skill Endpoint page

Code

Now that we have explored the **Build** section, let's jump to the Alexa service part, which is our Node.js code:

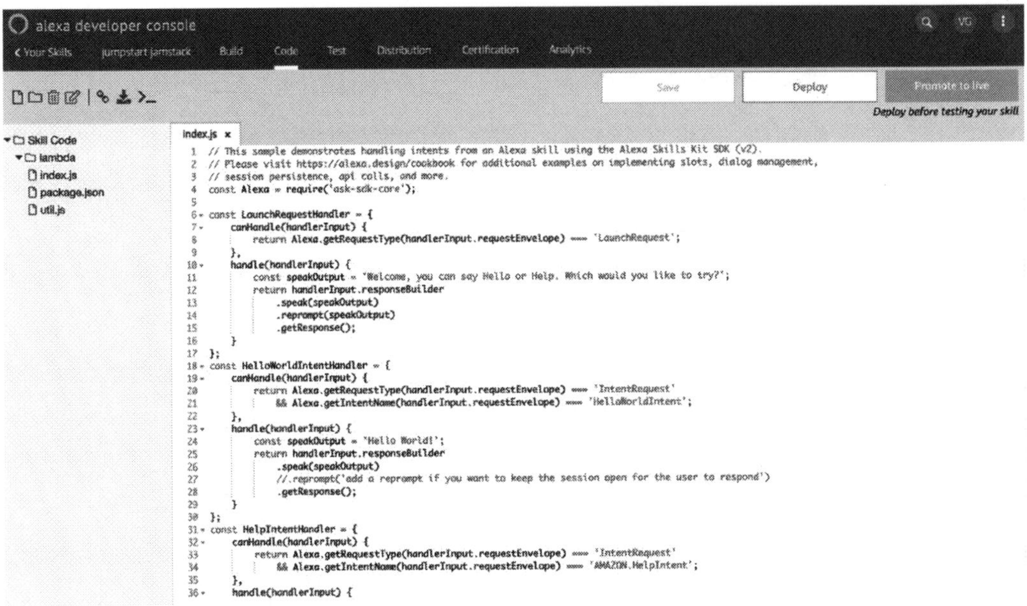

Figure 12.20 – Alexa skill Code page

As you can see, the interface provides a code editor where we can implement our Alexa service.

In our `index.js` file, we can create the handlers for our intent. Any new intent we add can be implemented here. Alexa provides an API to handle the request. It's called the `ask-sdk-core` API. The requests are inside the `handlerInput` JSON object.

The handler will process our intent and, from here, will make the Sanity call to our Sanity dataset.

At the top of our `index.js` file, we require `ask-sdk-core`:

```
const Alexa = require('ask-sdk-core');
```

The handler includes two functions: the `canHandle()` function checks whether this handler can process this request by checking the type of request, and the `handle()` function will process the request and return a response:

```
const MyCustomHandler = {
    canHandle(handlerInput) {
        return Alexa.getRequestType(handlerInput.
requestEnvelope) === 'MyRequestType' && Alexa.
getIntentName(handlerInput.requestEnvelope) === 'MyIntent';
    }
};
```

In our `canHandle()` function, we get the request type and the request name using the `ask-sdk-core` API.

If both conditions are true, it means that this handler can handle the request, so we implement the `handle()` function:

```
const MyCustomHandler = {
    canHandle(handlerInput) {
        return Alexa.getRequestType(handlerInput.
requestEnvelope) === 'MyRequestType' && Alexa.
getIntentName(handlerInput.requestEnvelope) === 'MyIntent';
    },
    handle(handlerInput) {
        const speakOutput = 'This is my custom text response';
        return handlerInput.responseBuilder
            .speak(speakOutput)
            .getResponse();
    }
};
```

In this simple example, we are just returning a text. The response we built using the `responseBuilder()` function passes the text to the `speak()` function and the `getResponse()` function will build the response.

The first handler we found in our file is `LaunchRequestHandler`. This handler is called when you open the skill with the command *Alexa, open jumpstart jamstack*:

```
const LaunchRequestHandler = {
    canHandle(handlerInput) {
        return Alexa.getRequestType(handlerInput.
requestEnvelope) === 'LaunchRequest';
    },
    handle(handlerInput) {
        const speakOutput = 'Welcome, you can say Hello or
Help. Which would you like to try?';
        return handlerInput.responseBuilder
            .speak(speakOutput)
            .reprompt(speakOutput)
            .getResponse();
    }
};
```

It will return the message, *Welcome, you can say Hello or Help. Which would you like to try?*

Let's change the message to make it related to our skill. Replace it with `Welcome to the jumpstart jamstack skill, and you can say, tell me the upcoming events or Help. Which would you like to try?`

So, our `LaunchRequest` handler will be as follows:

```
const LaunchRequestHandler = {
    canHandle(handlerInput) {
        return Alexa.getRequestType(handlerInput.
requestEnvelope) === 'LaunchRequest';
    },
    handle(handlerInput) {
        const speakOutput = 'Welcome to the jumpstart jamstack
skill, you can say tell me the upcoming events or Help. Which
would you like to try?';

        return handlerInput.responseBuilder
            .speak(speakOutput)
            .reprompt(speakOutput)
            .getResponse();
```

```
        }
};
```

Press the **Save** button above the editor:

Figure 12.21 – Alexa skill Code page

After that, we find `HelloWorldIntentHandler`. This is the custom handler that handles `HelloWorldIntent`, which is included in our skill by default:

```
const HelloWorldIntentHandler = {
    canHandle(handlerInput) {
        return Alexa.getRequestType(handlerInput.
requestEnvelope) === 'IntentRequest'
            && Alexa.getIntentName(handlerInput.
requestEnvelope) === 'HelloWorldIntent';
    },
    handle(handlerInput) {
        const speakOutput = 'Hello World!';
        return handlerInput.responseBuilder
            .speak(speakOutput)
            //.reprompt('add a reprompt if you want to keep the
session open for the user to respond')
            .getResponse();
    }
};
```

`HelpIntentHandler` provides a description of the skill to the user:

```
const HelpIntentHandler = {
    canHandle(handlerInput) {
        return Alexa.getRequestType(handlerInput.
requestEnvelope) === 'IntentRequest'
```

```
                && Alexa.getIntentName(handlerInput.
requestEnvelope) === 'AMAZON.HelpIntent';
    },
    handle(handlerInput) {
        const speakOutput = 'You can say hello to me! How can I
help?';

        return handlerInput.responseBuilder
            .speak(speakOutput)
            .reprompt(speakOutput)
            .getResponse();
    }
};
```

CancelAndStopIntent stops the skill. In this example, both intents are handled in the same way, but you can separate them into two separate handlers if you need to retrieve a different message back:

```
const CancelAndStopIntentHandler = {
    canHandle(handlerInput) {
        return Alexa.getRequestType(handlerInput.
requestEnvelope) === 'IntentRequest'
            && (Alexa.getIntentName(handlerInput.
requestEnvelope) === 'AMAZON.CancelIntent'
                || Alexa.getIntentName(handlerInput.
requestEnvelope) === 'AMAZON.StopIntent');
    },
    handle(handlerInput) {
        const speakOutput = 'Goodbye!';
        return handlerInput.responseBuilder
            .speak(speakOutput)
            .getResponse();
    }
};
```

`SessionEndedRequestHandler` is called when the intent is fulfilled and there is no `reprompt()` function in the response. It does not return any message:

```
const SessionEndedRequestHandler = {
    canHandle(handlerInput) {
        return Alexa.getRequestType(handlerInput.
requestEnvelope) === 'SessionEndedRequest';
    },
    handle(handlerInput) {
        // Any cleanup logic goes here.
        return handlerInput.responseBuilder.getResponse();
    }
};
```

`ErrorHandler` is called when an error occurs within your skill. It notifies the user with a message:

```
// Generic error handling to capture any syntax or routing
errors. If you receive an error
// stating the request handler chain is not found, you have not
implemented a handler for
// the intent being invoked or included it in the skill builder
below.
const ErrorHandler = {
    canHandle() {
        return true;
    },
    handle(handlerInput, error) {
        console.log(`~~~ Error handled: ${error.stack}`);
        const speakOutput = `Sorry, I had trouble doing what
you asked. Please try again.`;

        return handlerInput.responseBuilder
            .speak(speakOutput)
            .reprompt(speakOutput)
            .getResponse();
    }
};
```

At the end of the file, we export the handler using the `ask-sdk-core` API:

```
// The SkillBuilder acts as the entry point for your skill,
routing all request and response
// payloads to the handlers above. Make sure any new handlers
or interceptors you've
// defined are included below. The order matters - they're
processed top to bottom.
exports.handler = Alexa.SkillBuilders.custom()
    .addRequestHandlers(
        LaunchRequestHandler,
        HelloWorldIntentHandler,
        HelpIntentHandler,
        CancelAndStopIntentHandler,
        SessionEndedRequestHandler,
    )
    .addErrorHandlers(
        ErrorHandler,
    )
    .lambda();
```

Now, press the **Deploy** button above the editor to deploy our changes:

Figure 12.22 – Alexa skill Code page

Building our handler

Now we need to build our handler to get events from our Sanity Studio dataset. We will use the Sanity Client npm plugin as we did in *Chapter 11, APIs - Extending Gatsby*:

1. Go to npm to get the latest version of the package: `https://www.npmjs.com/package/@sanity/client`. You can see the version on the right-hand side of the page. At the time of writing this book, the latest stable version is **1.150.1**:

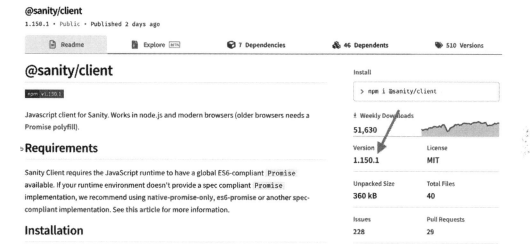

Figure 12.23 – NPM Sanity Client page

2. In our **Code** editor in our Alexa console, open the `package.json` file and add the Sanity Client npm plugin to the `dependencies` array:

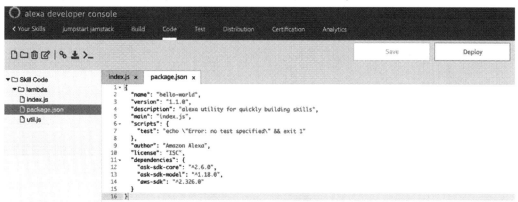

Figure 12.24 – Alexa skill Code page

3. Now, click on the **Save** button and then the **Deploy** button. Our package will be added automatically.

4. In the `index.js` page, after `HelloWorldIntentHandler`, we can add `GetUpcomingEventsIntentHandler`:

5. Let's start from the `canHandle()` function. We know that the request type must be an `IntentRequest` and that our intent name is `GetUpcomingEventsIntent`, so we write the following:

```
const GetUpcomingEventsIntentHandler = {
    canHandle(handlerInput) {
        return Alexa.getRequestType(handlerInput.
requestEnvelope) === 'IntentRequest'
            && Alexa.getIntentName(handlerInput.
requestEnvelope) === 'GetUpcomingEventsIntent';
    },
};
```

6. Now we can implement the `handle()` function. Because the Sanity Client returns a `Promise`, the `handle()` function must be asynchronous.

    The first step is to initialize the Sanity Client:

```
const GetUpcomingEventsIntentHandler = {
    canHandle(handlerInput) {
        ...
    }
    async handle(handlerInput) {
        const sanityClient = require('@sanity/client')
        const client = sanityClient({
            projectId: 'your-project-id',
            dataset: 'your-dataset',
            useCdn: true
        });
    }
};
```

7. Now we can fetch the data using the `fetch()` function from the Sanity Client API.

The fetch() function requires a **Graph Oriented Query** (**GROQ**). In our case, we want five documents of the event type where the event date is greater than the current date. We also prepare the list array where we can add our results and the speakOutput variable, where we can add the message. Then we use the fetch() function to get the results:

```
const GetUpcomingEventsIntentHandler = {
    canHandle(handlerInput) {
        ...
    }
    async handle(handlerInput) {
        const sanityClient = require('@sanity/client')
        const client = sanityClient({
            projectId: 'your-project-id',
            dataset: 'your-dataset',
            useCdn: true
        });
        const query = '*[_type == "event"]'
        let speakOutput
        let list = [];
        await client.fetch(query).then(events => {
            events.forEach(event => {
                list.push(event.name)
            })
        })
    }
};
```

Now, if there are upcoming events, they will be added to the list array.

8. We can now build the response:

```
const GetUpcomingEventsIntentHandler = {
    canHandle(handlerInput) {
        ...
    }
    async handle(handlerInput) {
        const sanityClient = require('@sanity/client')
        const client = sanityClient({
```

```
          projectId: 'your-project-id',
          dataset: 'your-dataset',
          useCdn: true
        });
. . .
        if (list.length > 0) {
            speakOutput = `I have found ${list.length}
events:  ${list.join(', ')}`;
        }
        else {
            speakOutput = ` I am sorry, there are not
upcoming events`;
        }
        return handlerInput.responseBuilder
            .speak(speakOutput)
            .getResponse();
    }
    }
};
```

9. The last part is to export our new handler,
    `GetUpcomingEventsIntentHandler`, to `exports.handler` at the bottom
    of the file:

```
exports.handler = Alexa.SkillBuilders.custom()
    .addRequestHandlers(
        ...
        GetUpcomingEventsIntentHandler,
        ...
    )
    .addErrorHandlers(
        ErrorHandler,
    )
    .lambda();
```

10. Now, press the **Save** and **Deploy** buttons above the editor.

At this point, we have created a new skill, configured the intents, and created the handler
for the intent. We are now ready to test our skill.

Test

If you want to test your skill, click on the **Test** link on the top menu:

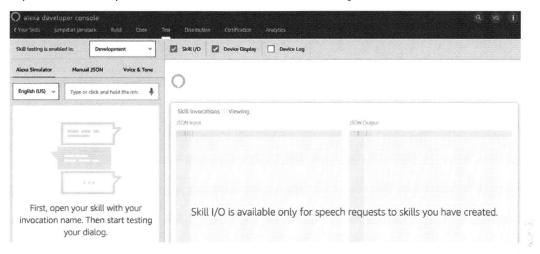

Figure 12.25 – Alexa skill Test page

From the left-hand side of the **Alexa Simulator** tab, you can speak or type your intent. Every skill has a launch request that can be called with the command `Alexa, open invocationName`. In our case, this will be *Alexa, open jumpstart jamstack*:

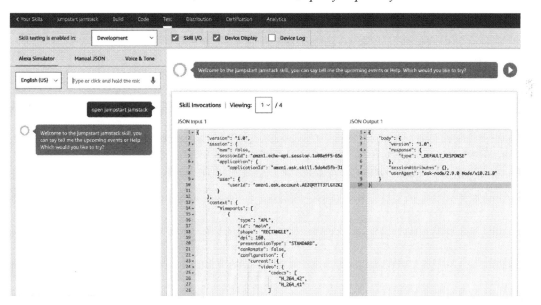

Figure 12.26 – Alexa skill Test page

As shown, we received a response from the launch request. In the **Skill Invocations** section, you can see the JSON input from the skill interface to the skill service.

Now, type the voice command in this way: `ask jumpstart jamstack to tell me the upcoming events` and examine the response.

Alexa will prompt the message containing five upcoming events:

Figure 12.27 – Alexa skill Test page

Summary

In this chapter, we went through the creation of an Alexa skill. We saw the difference between the skill interface and the skill service. We went through the component of an Alexa skill, and we have extended its functionality with a new command. We have also integrated our skill with our Sanity Studio. This means that our events are now reachable via a web application and via Alexa!

In the next chapter, we will return to our Gatsby application and explore the Tailwind CSS framework, which will help us to improve the visual aspect of our application.

13
Tying It All Together

In the last few chapters, we learned about the ways in which our web application can interact with third-party systems. Now, we'll return to our web application and improve the visual aspects of the website to make the user interface modern and more appealing.

First, we'll start by modifying the styles by importing new **Cascading Style Sheets** (CSS). Then, we'll clean up the index page code and adjust some of the various final elements of the website. By doing this, we're approaching the time to deploy the website.

The main topics that we will cover in this chapter are as follows:

- Gatsby.js layout modifications
- Preparing for deployment

Technical requirements

To deploy the project on Netlify, you must have an account at `https://www.netlify.com/`. To deploy the project on Azure, you must create an account at `https://azure.microsoft.com/en-us/`.

Additionally, a terminal program is needed.

Gatsby.js layout modifications

There are many different ways to incorporate styles into a web page to change the default fonts, colors, backgrounds, and layout. While style and classes can also be created one by one, an easier and more efficient approach is to use a framework to leverage pre-built ideas and design patterns. One of the hottest cascading frameworks at the time of writing is Tailwind CSS. Let's introduce Tailwind and learn why it is used within Gatsby.

Introducing Tailwind CSS

Tailwind CSS is a nice CSS framework that is easy to learn and use. It aims to be unopinionated and is driven toward allow the designer to construct styles from smaller pieces. Let's start by installing the framework so that we can use it.

Installing the Tailwind CSS framework

We will install it and use it to improve the visual appearance of the website:

1. The first step is to use the Node package manager to install Tailwind CSS. In the terminal, type the following command:

    ```
    npm install tailwindcss --save-dev
    ```

    The `--save-dev` argument will add it to the project's development dependencies. Additionally, since we want to improve the appearance of the form, we will add an additional package built by Tailwind Labs called `custom-forms`.

2. Again, we'll add this to the project's development properties. Type the following command into the terminal as well:

    ```
    npm install @tailwindcss/custom-forms --save-dev
    ```

3. Finally, by typing the following command in to the terminal, the configuration file is automatically created:

    ```
    npx tailwindcss init
    ```

The `tailwind.config.js` file gets created in Gatsby's main folder, in the `/web` directory. This file contains the Tailwind configuration. The contents of the file are composed as follows:

```
module.exports = {
  purge: [],
  theme: {
    extend: {}
  },
  variants: {},
  plugins: [require('@tailwindcss/custom-forms')]
}
```

Most of the options use the default settings, and hence they are empty. The only option used is the list of plugins. Here, the list of plugins only includes the `custom-forms` plugin, which we installed previously.

Using the Tailwind CSS framework

Next, we'll integrate the Tailwind framework into the project. Starting with the `web/src/styles/layout.css` file, we need to insert the following lines of code. The following lines of code will bring Tailwind's styles into the project:

```
@tailwind base;
@tailwind components;
@tailwind utilities;
```

Formatting the event proposal form

Revisiting the event proposal form of our project's website, it's obvious that there is no style at all. So, let's first review the form's code. The following is an excerpt of the HTML source code for the event title input and label:

```
<div className='field'>
  <label className='label'>Event Title:
    <input className='input' type='text' name='eventTitle'/>
  </label>
</div>
```

Using Tailwind CSS, the form has been styled as shown in the following figure:

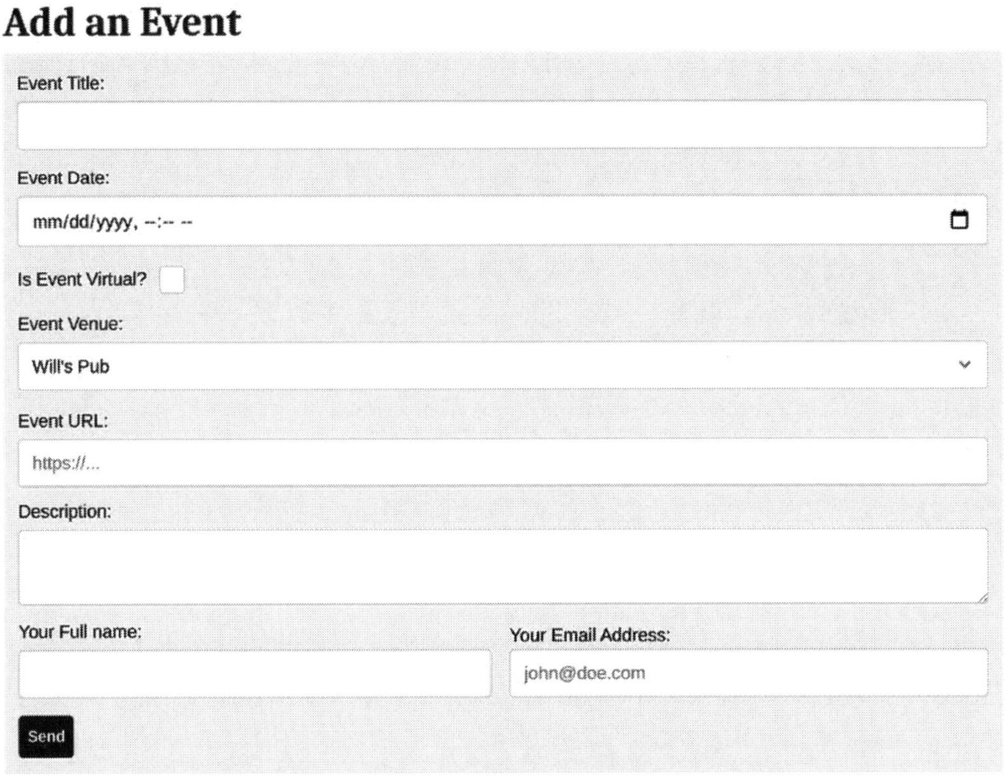

Add an Event

Event Title:

Event Date:

mm/dd/yyyy, --:-- --

Is Event Virtual?

Event Venue:

Will's Pub

Event URL:

https://...

Description:

Your Full name:

Your Email Address:

john@doe.com

Send

Figure 13.1 – The event proposal form styled with Tailwind

> **Note**
> The full documentation for Tailwind CSS can be found at
> `https://tailwindcss.com`.

For the purpose of this book, we'll look at the following example, which is simply one small component of the full capabilities of Tailwind CSS. Here, we have the previous HTML code block now styled with Tailwind:

```
<div className='mt-10 block'>
    <label className='label'>Event Title:
        <input className='form-input mt-1 block w-full' type='text'
name='eventTitle'/>
    </label>
</div>
```

First, a space was added around each form element. Let's quickly review what types of options exist to add space around an element. Each element in the HTML **Document Object Model (DOM)** has three surrounding components: the border, the margin, and the padding. In the simplest terms, `margin` is the spacing around an element and `padding` is the spacing inside of an element. `border`, as the name would suggest, is any of several ways to visually delineate an HTML element.

The first of the *styles* we'll examine is `mt-10`. This nomenclature is a bit different than in other CSS frameworks since both the `m` and the `t` have an atomic meaning.

The `m` in Tailwind represents `margin`. Likewise, `p` is used for `padding`, `t` represents `top`, and so obviously, `b` represents `bottom`, `r` is `right`, and `l` is `left`. Additionally, `y` represents both the top and bottom, and `x` represents both the right and left sides. If `m` and `p` are used alone (`m-10`, for example), this usage represents the entire element, so space would be provided on all sides. This makes remembering which attribute to use quite easy, lending to the framework's popularity.

`-10` represents 10 pixels. This will provide 10 pixels of needed space at the top of each form element to provide a cleaner appearance.

Additionally, the Tailwind CSS `block` style is used to set a block-style layout.

For the form input element, a text box, in this case, with the Tailwind `form-input` style, is used. This applies the following styles:

- `background-color: #fff;`: White
- `border-color: #e2e8f0; border-width: 1px; border-radius: 0.25rem;`: A lightly colored, 1-pixel input border with slightly rounded edges
- `padding-right: 0.75rem; padding-left: 0.75rem;`: More space around the sides of the text
- `padding-top: 0.5rem; padding-bottom: 0.5rem;`: More space around the top and bottom of the text
- `line-height: 1.5;`: Sets the vertical text spacing
- `font-size: 1rem;`: Sets the text size

The `w-full` form input style instructs the form element to be at the full width of its container. As shown in the form, the **Your Full Name** and **Your Email Address** fields are half-width. Since the form should be responsive, the full width is used for these elements when the form is small, for example, when the browser is minimized horizontally, such as when a smartphone is used for viewing it. The following two styles work together to make this happen: `sm:w-full` and `md:w-1/2`.

The width of the element will be full when the form container is in small mode and half-width (1/2) when the form is at least medium size, or the browser width is greater than 768 pixels wide.

Improving and formatting the event list

In the previous section, we added Tailwind styles to the event proposal form. Next, we can add styles to the list of events on the website. In the following figure, *Figure 13.2*, the events list is shown with Tailwind CSS styles also applied to the list of events:

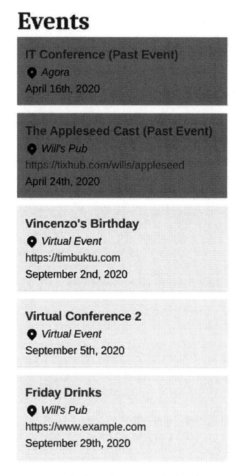

Figure 13.2 – The list of events styled with Tailwind

By adding sorting to the events query, the events are listed in chronological order. The following code demonstrates how this is done. Sorting is added to the `dateAndTime` field using the `ASC` (ascending) order:

```
events: allSanityEvent(
  sort: {
    fields: [dateAndTime]

    order: ASC
  },
) {
  ...
```

As shown in *Figure 13.2*, events that happened in the past, prior to September 1, 2020, in this case, are displayed with a darker background than events that will happen in the future. Let's learn how this effect is achieved.

First, `node.dateAndTime` is converted into a date by passing it as a parameter to the new `Date()` function. The current time is obtained by instantiating a `date` object without a parameter. The Boolean (`true/false`) result of the comparison, if the event date is less than the current date, is assigned to the `pastEvent` variable:

```
let pastEvent =
new Date(node.dateAndTime) < new Date() ? true : false;
```

Next, the background color is set based on whether `pastEvent`'s value is set to `True`:

```
(${pastEvent ? 'bg-gray-600' : 'bg-gray-100'}):
return (
  <div className={`max-w-full shadow-sm mt-3 p-3 ${pastEvent ?
  'bg-gray-600' : 'bg-gray-100'}`}>
  ...
```

Now that we've dealt with the styles, next, we will look at how to improve the code quality. We'll begin to prepare for deployment by first cleaning up the source code.

Preparing for deployment

In this section, we will make several improvements to the code, making it cleaner. Additionally, we will improve the functionality of the form.

Cleaning up the code

Since the list of events and the event form source code could eventually be reused in multiple places on the website, we can refactor the code by creating separate components for each.

In the web/src/components folder, create two files: event-list.js and event-form.js. Both files are similar in format.

The basic format of the event list module is as shown in the following code block:

```
import {Link} from "gatsby";
import React from "react";
const {format} = require('date-fns')


function EventList(props) {

    return (

    ...

    )

}



EventList.defaultProps = {
    title: '',
    eventNodes: [],
}


export default EventList
```

The basic format of the event form module is as shown:

```
import React from "react";

function EventForm(props) {
    return (

    ...

    )

}
```

```
EventForm.defaultProps = {
  title: '',
  venueNodes: [],
}

export default EventForm
```

The source code of the event form and event list will be inserted into `return`. Opening and closing `<div>` tags are added since JSX requires a root node:

```
return (
  <div>
    <h2 className='font-serif text-4xl font-bold text-gray-800
bb-10'>{props.title}</h2>
    <div className='max-w-full'>
    ...
  </div>
)
```

To use the two newly created components, they need to be imported:

```
import EventList from '../components/event-list'
import EventForm from '../components/event-form'
```

Now, the event list and event form may be replaced with these components. The nodes and title will be passed into these components as properties:

```
<EventList
  eventNodes={eventNodes}
  title='Events'
/>


<EventForm
  venueNodes={venueNodes}
  title='Add an Event'
/>
```

Remember, now the nodes and the titles are passed in as `props`. Previously, the events and venues were able to be used directly from the GraphQL result as follows:

```
{eventNodes && eventNodes.map((node) => (
```

Now, the nodes will be accessed through `props`:

```
{props.eventNodes && props.eventNodes.map((venue) => (
```

Similarly, `title` is now passed in as a property, so the code should be refactored as follows:

```
<h2 className='font-serif text-4xl font-bold text-gray-800 bb-10'>{props.title}</h2>
```

Now that the code has been improved, we can improve the form by leveraging one of React's features to improve the user experience.

Toggling the venue visibility

When the event is virtual, it would be nice to hide the venue selector, since it isn't relevant.

To do this, we'll need to utilize React Hooks by adding it to `import React` in `event-form.js` as shown:

```
import React, {useState} from "react";
```

The new feature that we'll use in this section is `useState()`, so let's look at its definition.

From the documentation, `useState()` *returns a stateful value, and a function to update it.*

In our case, `isVisible` is the Boolean stateful value and `toggleVisible` is the function to update it, as shown:

```
function EventForm(props) {
    const [isVisible, toggleVisible] = useState(true)
```

The two `<div>` elements should be modified as follows:

```
<div className='mt-10 block'>
    <label className=''>Is Event Virtual?
        <input onClick={() => toggleVisible(!isVisible)}
className='form-checkbox ml-3 h-6 w-6'
        type='checkbox' name='virtual'/>
```

```
      </label>
    </div>

<div className='mt-10 block'>
  {isVisible && <label className=''>Event Venue:
    <select className='form-select block w-full mt-1'
name='venue' id={`venue`}>
      {props.venueNodes &&
      props.venueNodes.map((venue) => (
        <option value={venue._id}>{venue.name}</option>
      ))}
    </select>
  </label>
  }
</div>
```

The HTML `onClick` event attribute is added to the toggle input, passing the opposite value (!) of the `isVisible` Boolean variable:

```
onClick={() => toggleVisible(!isVisible)}
```

If `isVisible` evaluates as `true`, then the event venue selection and label are shown; otherwise, they're hidden.

Summary

In this chapter, we learned how to style a website for modern design and responsiveness using the Tailwind CSS framework, saving time and effort when compared to starting with traditional CSS. Next, we learned how to extract fragments of the page into separate components. Finally, we added dynamic functionality to the form itself.

Styling and polishing the user experience is a deep subject, and therefore beyond the scope of this book. Feel free to read the Tailwind CSS documentation for more ways to improve the appearance. Also, even using other elements of React, which Gatsby can fully take advantage of, could help build out this prototype into a full website—you have all the tools needed.

In the next chapter, Netlify will be used to deploy the website and we will see its usefulness in automating many tasks that previously needed to be performed manually.

14

Deployment Using Netlify and Azure

In the last chapter, we prepared our website for deployment. We added style to the components using Tailwind CSS. Lastly, we cleaned up the layout and refactored the code to components. Now, we can look more closely at the last component of the Jamstack used in this book: **Netlify**. Netlify is used as the default platform for the *Blog with Gatsby* example that was created at `https://sanity.io/create`. At the time of writing this book, Microsoft has added the Static Web Apps service, providing yet another option for deployment. Since GitHub and Azure are both owned by Microsoft, there is an excellent integration between the Static Web Apps service and GitHub.

This chapter first introduces the Netlify serverless continuous deployment hosting service, which automates many of the tasks that previously either needed to be developed or performed manually, and then demonstrates Azure Static Web Apps as an alternative for developers who may already be using Azure or who want to try this new service.

The main topics that we will cover in this chapter are the following:

- Introduction to Netlify
- Netlify plugins
- Advanced configuration through the `netlify.toml` file
- Netlify deployment via the command line
- Azure Static Web Apps deployment

Technical requirements

To deploy the project on Netlify, you must have an account at `https://www.netlify.com/`. To deploy the project on Azure, you must create an account at `https://azure.microsoft.com/en-us/`.

Additionally, a Terminal program is needed.

Introduction to Netlify

Netlify, to someone who is new to web development, initially looks like a deployment and hosting platform.

In fact, a Netlify website can be a simple static file web host. Using Netlify's drag and drop feature, a folder of web files can be deployed as a real, functional, and hosted website in seconds, as shown:

Want to deploy a new site without connecting to Git?
Drag and drop your site folder here

Figure 14.1 – Netlify's drag and drop deployment interface

However, while it is a place to host your website, it is so much more than that.

Firstly, behind the scenes, when we initially created our Sanity and Gatsby-generated website, the code provided by Sanity and Gatsby Blog Template automatically runs it, thereby creating an integration between Sanity and Netlify.

Both Sanity Studio and the Gatsby-generated website were immediately built and hosted on Netlify's server, and new versions of the website could be easily and automatically deployed as often as we wish. Through integration connecting Sanity's management tool and Netlify, a new version of the website can be built when we change the contents within Sanity. Also, there is a *hook* or a *trigger* set up through GitHub that will automatically deploy a new version of the website whenever the Gatsby source code is pushed to GitHub.

Secondly, Netlify is a serverless continuous delivery service built on top of **Amazon Web Services (AWS)**. This means that all the infrastructure provided by AWS is automatically built into Netlify's hosting ability. This means that there are servers located throughout the world, also referred to as *the cloud*, that deliver content in the fastest way possible to all website users.

However, these two aspects are just the beginning of the story. Netlify can run many different types of code together through scripts, in several languages, during the build process to enhance your website, as shown in the following screenshot:

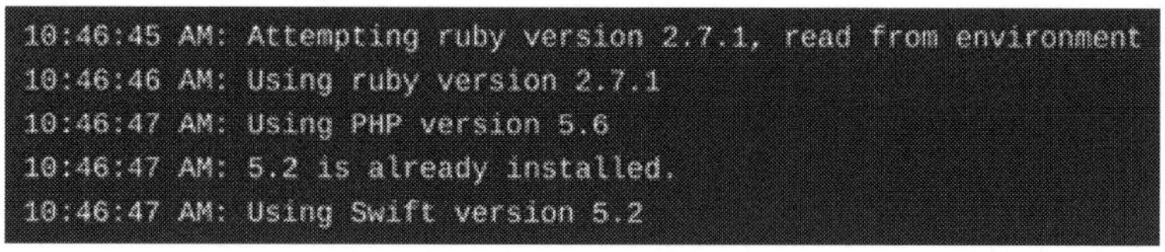

```
10:46:45 AM: Attempting ruby version 2.7.1, read from environment
10:46:46 AM: Using ruby version 2.7.1
10:46:47 AM: Using PHP version 5.6
10:46:47 AM: 5.2 is already installed.
10:46:47 AM: Using Swift version 5.2
```

Figure 14.2 – An excerpt of Netlify's build output

This is useful when there are pre-built pieces of code that are needed to build the static pages. For example, the PHP programming language can be used to extract or preprocess format data or even generate websites statically. Hence, the JavaScript programming language is not the only option during deployment.

It is important to remember that code can only be run on Netlify at the time of deployment. Hence, a traditional content management system such as WordPress cannot run on Netlify since it requires server-side code to run on each page request.

One nice feature is the ability to do an A/B test. This is accomplished by using two branches in GitHub. Let's imagine that you would like to test the effect a particular color has on the performance of a button that website visitors need to click. You could have two different branches in GitHub configuring Netlify to randomly select one or the other.

Another feature that Netlify provides is an easy way to insert code snippets into the header or body of a page. One example of this usage would be pasting the code snippet required for Google Analytics to work properly in the page.

Next, let's learn about ways to take advantage of what Netlify has to offer though their plugins.

Netlify plugins

Netlify's plugin library automates many manual processes and saves developers the effort of having to develop in-house solutions. This growing library includes many plugins. For example, one plugin can fetch and incorporate external resources such as RSS feeds. Another plugin can also generate a sitemap or even index the website content to create a search functionality.

HTML Minify

The plugin that we'll examine for the purpose of this book compresses the HTML, reducing the file size by removing unnecessary page or code contents, or substituting variable names with single-character replacements. This process is called **minification**.

We would like to Minify the HTML code as much as possible, so we could use Netlify's plugin called `netlify-plugin-minify-html` to compress the file contents. When Gatsby builds the static pages, it minimizes the content of the HTML files.

The following is an example of how the readable source code would appear prior to minification:

```
<h1 hidden="">
  Welcome to <!-- -->My new blog
</h1>
<div class="blog-post-preview-list-module--root--2LgdR">
    <h2 class="blog-post-preview-list-module--headline--3j8kB">
  Latest blog posts
</h2>
....
```

Once minification is performed, the total file size is reduced. Here is how the HTML code appears following minification:

```
<h1 hidden="">Welcome to <!-- -->My new blog</h1><div
class="blog-post-preview-list-module--root--2LgdR"><h2
class="blog-post-preview-list-module--headline--3j8kB">Latest
blog posts</h2>
```

Extra spaces have been removed, but the `netlify-plugin-minify-html` file is able to make the file size even smaller. Every character counts toward the total amount of data on the page that needs to be transferred over the internet, so this is a wonderful feature.

The following steps will activate the Netlify Minify plugin:

1. Log in to `https://netlify.com`. In the horizontal menu underneath the website name, click on the **Plugins** link:

Figure 14.3 – The horizontal menu

2. Locate the Minify HTML plugin and click on the gray **Install** button.

3. Then, choose the project website (the name usually ends in -web):

Install Minify HTML plugin

A plugin to add HTML minification as a post-processing optimisation in Netlify

1. Select site to install plugin

Where do you want to install Minify HTML plugin?

Choose a site where you'd like to use this plugin.

    Q Search sites

Figure 14.4 – The Netlify Minify plugin installation screen

4. When asked **Are you sure you want to install Minify HTML**, click the green **Install** button.

    Now, at this point, the Netlify web interface should return you to the plugins page for the website. **Minify HTML** should be displayed.

5. Next, in the horizontal menu underneath the website name, click on the **Deploys** link.

6. On the right side of the interface, click on the gray **Trigger deploy** button, which will display a menu, and then the **Deploy site** menu item, as shown in *Figure 14.5*:

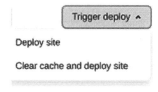

Figure 14.5 – The Trigger deploy menu

This will build and deploy a new version of the website. The **Deploy in Progress** page will display a log where the output will be displayed.

The log output is extremely useful for learning about what is performed during deployment and whether there are any warnings or errors. The Netlify deployment will be stopped if there are any errors to ensure that no website will be deployed.

The following is the code once Netlify Minify HTML is executed:

```
<h1 hidden>Welcome to My new blog</h1><div class=blog-post-
  preview-list-module--root--2LgdR><h2 class=blog-post-preview-
  list-module--headline--3j8kB>Latest blog posts</h2>
```

Compare this to the minified code earlier in this chapter. Netlify Minify HTML removes the quotation marks when the HTML tag attribute is a continuous string (without spaces) and also removes comments, so < ! - - - - > is removed. The final result is a smaller file. This is just one example of the many ways whereby, as a result of using Netlify plugins, we can improve the resultant static content and enhance its functionality. Exploring the plugins will open up many new possibilities.

Next, we will begin to explore, more deeply, the configuration options available for Netlify's features.

Advanced configuration through the netlify. toml file

While the Netlify web interface is easy to use, for more control over the deployment process, a `netlify.toml` file can be used, which uses *Tom's Obvious, Minimal Language* format.

Let's now learn how to create and use this configuration file to access the advanced features of Netlify.

Create a file in the project's root directory named `netlify.toml`. Here is an example of the file contents:

```
[[plugins]]
  package = "netlify-plugin-minify-html"


  # Specify which deploy contexts we'll minify HTML in.
  # Supports any Deploy Contexts available in Netlify.
  # https://docs.netlify.com/site-deploys/overview/#deploy-
  contexts
  [plugins.inputs]
    contexts = [
```

```
        'production',
        'branch-deploy',
        'deploy-preview'
    ]

    [plugins.inputs.minifierOptions]
      removeComments = false
      collapseInlineTagWhitespace = false
```

The [[plugins]] annotation is used for each plugin. Next, [plugins.inputs] is used to determine the contexts for which the plugin will be activated. For example, when developing locally, Minify is usually not required, so the plugin will only be triggered in just the production and preview contexts.

Next, the [plugins.inputs.minifierOptions] section of the plugin configuration allows us to customize the plugin even more. Since, by default, removeComments is set to true, this option can be set to false by using the removeComments = false option.

We may use the Netlify command-line tool once again, but this time by typing the following command in the project's root directory:

```
netlify build
```

The preceding command triggers the build locally, combining the netlify.toml configuration and the plugins that are configured in Netlify's plugin list for the website.

Here is the relevant excerpt from the output of netlify build:

```
┌─────────────────────────────────────────────────────┐
| 2. onSuccess command from netlify-plugin-minify-html |
└─────────────────────────────────────────────────────┘

Minifiying HTML in the deploy context: production
Minifiying HTML with these options: { removeComments: false }

(netlify-plugin-minify-html onSuccess completed in 259ms)

┌─────────────────────────────┐
|    Netlify Build Complete    |
└─────────────────────────────┘

(Netlify Build completed in 19.8s)
```

In this section, we've learned how to use the Netlify configuration file. Next, we will learn how to build and deploy Netlify using the command line.

Netlify deployment via the command line

Netlify's command-line tool also provides a nice way to preview the site without deploying it once the `netlify build` command is run.

In the Terminal, type the following command:

```
netlify deploy
```

The output will be similar to the following:

```
Deploy path:            /home/chris/jumpstart-jamstack/web/public
Configuration path: /home/chris/jumpstart-jamstack /netlify.
toml
Deploying to draft URL...
Finished hashing 49 files
CDN requesting 0 files
Finished uploading 0 assets
Draft deploy is live!


Logs:                   https://app.netlify.com/sites/jumpstart-
jamstack-web/deploys/5f3cad51bdd06713f5250887
Website Draft URL: https://5f3cad51bdd06713f5250887--jumpstart-
jamstack-web.netlify.app


If everything looks good on your draft URL, deploy it to your
main site URL with the --prod flag.
netlify deploy --prod
```

As the command's output reveals, a `Draft deploy` preview URL is made available so that the production website may be viewed without deploying it. In the example, this is `https://5f3cad51bdd06713f5250887--jumpstart-jamstack-web.netlify.app`.

`--open` is another useful flag that can be added. This will open the URL in the default browser. The relevant command would be as follows:

```
netlify deploy --open
```

Finally, as the output also states, by adding the `--prod` flag, `deploy` will be deployed and replace the current version in production if the deployment succeeds.

```
netlify deploy --prod
```

Additionally, in order to open the URL in the browser, add the `--open` flag as before:

```
netlify deploy --prod -open
```

The output from this command will be similar to the following:

```
Deploy path:           /home/chris/jumpstart-jamstack/hands-on-
jamstack/web/public
Configuration path: /home/chris/jumpstart-jamstack/hands-on-
jamstack/netlify.toml
Deploying to main site URL...
Finished hashing 1 files
CDN requesting 0 files
Finished uploading 0 assets
Deploy is live!

Logs:                  https://app.netlify.com/sites/jumpstart-
jamstack-web/deploys/5f3cb84fbdd067963e250875
Unique Deploy URL: https://5f3cb84fbdd067963e250875--jumpstart-
jamstack-web.netlify.app
Website URL:           https://jumpstart-jamstack-web.netlify.app
```

`Unique Deploy URL` provides a way to *rollback* to this particular deployment in the future, while `Website URL`, as expected, is the newly deployed *version* of the website.

In this section, we have learned how to build and deploy on Netlify using the command line. Next, we will learn another way to deploy Jamstack websites using Azure.

Azure Static Web Apps deployment

A preview of the Azure Static Web Apps service was introduced, placing yet another competitor in the Jamstack hosting and deployment space. The URL to try out this service can be found at `https://azure.microsoft.com/en-us/services/app-service/static/`.

Static web app creation

To create a static web app using Azure, follow these steps in order:

1. Start by creating an Azure account. The steps for creating a free Azure account may vary depending on the country. The following URL may take you to the signup page for your country: `https://azure.microsoft.com/free/`.

2. After signup, you should eventually arrive at the Azure portal location (`https://portal.azure.com/`). Here is a screenshot of the top navigation of this screen:

Figure 14.6 – The Azure portal top navigation

The various Azure services are listed. As shown in *Figure 14.6*, **Static Web Apps (Preview)** is one of the options.

3. Placing the mouse on the **Static Web Apps (Preview)** button, the following menu will be displayed:

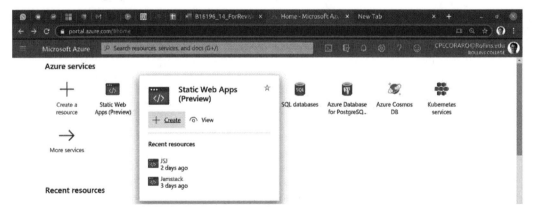

Figure 14.7 – Static Web Apps creation

4. Click on **Create** to create the Jamstack app.

5. Next, we will fill in the project details, **Static Web App details**, and **Source Control Details** fields:

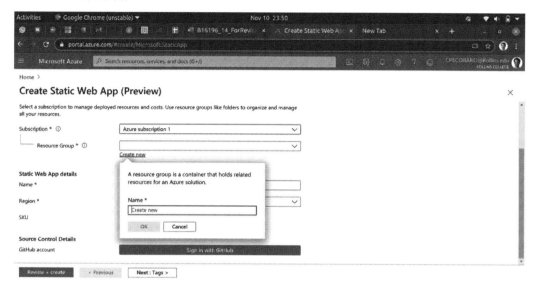

Figure 14.8 – Resource Group creation

6. Create a new resource group, enter a name for the static app, and then select an appropriate region.

7. Next, for **Source Control Details**, click the blue **Sign in with GitHub** button to sign in to your GitHub account. Authorize Azure to access your GitHub account.

8. In **Source Control Details**, choose your GitHub account name for **Organization**, and the appropriate **Branch**, which is usually the **master**:

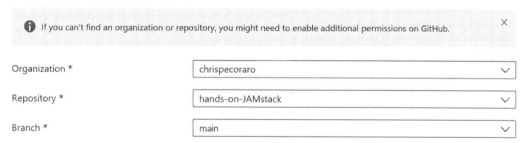

Figure 14.9 – Organization, Repository, and Branch selection on the configuration form

9. Finally, in the **Build Details** section, for the **Build Presets** option, select **Gatsby** in the **Static site generator** section:

Create Static Web App (Preview)

Repository *	jumpstart-jamstack ⌄

Branch *	production ⌄

Build Details

Enter values to create a GitHub Actions workflow file for build and release. You can modify the workflow file later in your GitHub repository.

Build Presets	Gatsby ⌄

ⓘ These fields will reflect the app type's default project structure. Change the values to suit your app.

App location * ⓘ	/

Api location ⓘ	api

App artifact location ⓘ	public

Figure 14.10 – Build Details and Build Presets selection on the configuration form

10. Lastly, and most importantly, set the **App location** to `/web/` since that is where the Gatsby application is located in our project. **Api location** is to be left blank (delete `api`).

11. At the bottom, click the **Review + create** button, followed by the blue **Create** button. If everything is correct, the static website should be deployed. The deployment begins as queued and then begins building, so the entire process requires a few minutes:

Create Static Web App (Preview)

Basics   Tags   Review + create

App Service Static Web Apps is a streamlined, highly efficient solution to take your static app from source code to global high availability. Pre-rendered files are served from a global footprint with no web servers required. Learn more ☑

Project Details

Select a subscription to manage deployed resources and costs. Use resource groups like folders to organize and manage all your resources.

Subscription * ⓘ | Azure subscription No technical support   ⌄ |

⌐ —— Resource Group * ⓘ | (New) JumpstartJamstack   ⌄ |
                                     Create new

Static Web App details

Name * | JSJ   ✓ |

Region * | East US 2   ⌄ |

SKU   Free

Source Control Details

GitHub account   chrispecoraro

> ⓘ If you can't find an organization or repository, you might need to enable additional permissions on GitHub.   ✕

Organization * | chrispecoraro   ⌄ |

Repository * | jumpstart-jamstack   ⌄ |

Branch * | production   ⌄ |

Build Details

Enter values to create a GitHub Actions workflow file for build and release. You can modify the workflow file later in your GitHub repository.

Build Presets | Gatsby   ⌄ |

                                    ⓘ These fields will reflect the app type's default project structure. Change the values to suit your app.

App location * ⓘ | /web   ✓ |

Api location ⓘ | e.g. "api", "functions", etc... |

Output location ⓘ | public |

Build Presets | Gatsby   ⌄ |

                                    ⓘ These fields will reflect the app type's default project structure. Change the values to suit your app.

App location * ⓘ | /web   ✓ |

Api location ⓘ | e.g. "api", "functions", etc... |

Output location ⓘ | public |

[Review + create]   [< Previous]   [Next : Tags >]

Figure 14.11 – A completed Azure Static Web Apps service configuration form

Static web app continuous deployment

Following deployment of the static web app, the screen shown in *Figure 14.12* is displayed:

1. Clicking on the blue **Go to resource** button takes us to the **Essentials** screen:

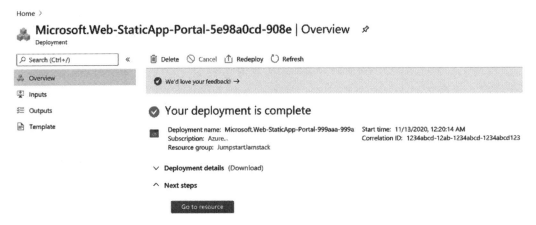

Figure 14.12 – The Azure Static Web Apps service deployment confirmation screen

2. The **Essentials** screen, which is accessed from the **Overview** menu item on the left-hand menu, displays the following information:

    Resource group

    Location (region)

    Subscription and **Subscription ID**

    Tags, if applicable

    URL, which can be clicked to access the static web app

    Source, which is the deployed GitHub branch, **schema** in this case

    Deployment history, which is used to access the deployments from GitHub

Edit workflow, which is used to edit the text-based workflow file in `.yml` format:

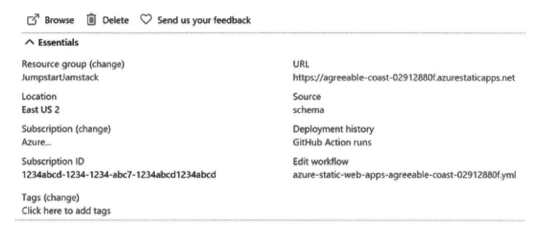

Figure 14.13 – The Azure Static Web Apps service Essentials screen

3. Clicking on the URL or, alternatively, the **Browse** button in the top menu will launch the web application in the browser.

4. Clicking on **GitHub Action runs** will lead us to the **Workflows** screen, as shown in *Figure 14.14*:

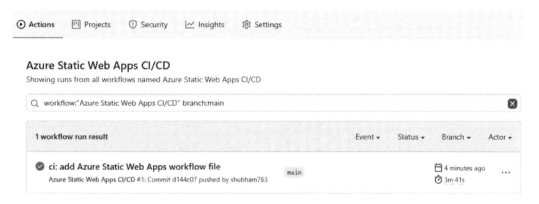

Figure 14.14 – The Azure Static Web Apps CI/CD screen

All the deployments are displayed in the preceding screenshot.

5. Clicking on the **Azure Static Web Apps CI/CD** link (beginning with **ci:**) will bring us to the management screen to view the deployment details for that workflow:

Figure 14.15 – A collapsed view of the Build and Deploy job screen

In the left menu, by clicking on the **Build and Deploy** job link, the details of the deployment may be viewed as shown in *Figure 14.16*:

The following screenshot shows what an expanded view looks like:

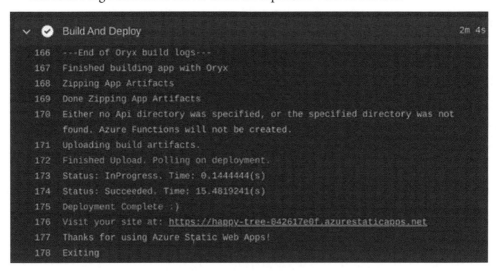

Figure 14.16 – Excerpt of the expanded view of the Build and Deploy job screen

In the expanded view of the **Build and Deploy** tab, the actual output of the deployment is shown. The text is nicely colored red, yellow, and green to show warnings and success messages.

While, at time of writing, the Static Web Apps service on Azure is still a preview release, it definitely demonstrates a viable alternative to Netlify.

Summary

In this chapter, we learned how to deploy websites through Netlify. We also learned how to install and use Netlify plugins, as well as how to use the `netlify.toml` configuration file and command-line utilities.

Additionally, we learned how to create and manage a Jamstack web application through the Static Web Apps service on Azure and also how to manage app redeployments through GitHub.

Having multiple options for Jamstack deployment demonstrates its decoupled nature. Multiple services can be easily leveraged for the same application, as needed.

In the next chapter, we will conclude our journey into the world of Jamstack and discuss the present and future state of the Jamstack community, other tools and alternative components of the ecosystem, and upcoming technologies and companies that are writing the future.

15
Conclusion

This closing chapter summarizes the concepts learned throughout the book and how the Jamstack community is evolving. The chapter will discuss the various external projects and how to contribute to them. The main topics that we will cover in this chapter are as follows:

- The Jamstack's future
- The Jamstack community resources
- Contributing to Jamstack projects

Summary of concepts

We began with an outline of the history of web development, showing how dynamic technology, such as *Server Side Includes*, eventually worked its way into static pages, adding functionality. These techniques, while adding more dynamicity, eventually led to server-side heaviness, increasing load time. Next, we introduced Sanity, a content delivery platform, and Sanity Studio, as a decoupled way to manage content, abandoning the monolithic approach that was pervasive for many years. Then we showed how its proprietary query language, GROQ, created an easy and terse way to interact with content and Sanity schemas.

Next, we compared GROQ with the familiar **Standard Query Language (SQL)**. We introduced GraphQL, as a new way to query content as a specification, breaking away from RESTful. We introduced the GraphQL Playground as a way to easily and quickly create GraqhQL queries and visualize results.

Next, we introduced Gatsby, a framework for creating websites and apps, showing how, through its extensive collection of plugins, it is able to source multiple pieces of data, such as files on the filesystem, Sanity, and other headless content management systems such as Drupal. We showed how Gatsby can use GraphQL to source content from the content source, such as with Sanity. We learned how to create parts of pages using underlying React framework components and how they work together to generate pages. We learned how Gatsby integrates cascading style sheets using CSS frameworks such as Tailwind. We also showed how Alexa can integrate with Sanity, enabling speech-to-text on Amazon devices.

Lastly, we learned how to use the powerful Netlify continuous delivery cloud-based hosting platform. We learned how it connects to GitHub and can automatically deploy a website whenever updates are made to its source code and how to use its collection of plugins to minify content, generate site maps, and even launch testing tools, such as Lighthouse.

Now, let's take a quick look at the Jamstack ecosystem, and learn about a few of the exciting upcoming events and features on its various platforms.

The Jamstack's future

The growth of the Jamstack, at the time of writing, is very evident. In the next section, we'll learn about some of the new technologies and trends emerging within the community.

Jamstack, JAMstack, and JAM Stack

We hope that you have enjoyed reading this book. There are many topics we would have liked to have covered, because the Jamstack is a constantly evolving concept. Many of the code examples may be improved upon as the various frameworks mature and newer versions are released. We wrote this book split between two time zones, one in the United States and one in Europe. We also wrote this book during a difficult time in the history of the world, when a pandemic caused massive lockdowns.

Despite these difficulties, we have shown that technical collaboration is possible in any situation. In fact, the state of the art regarding cloud-based and networking technology has been pushed to its limits. It has, in a way, been brought to the forefront, both in the news and in many industries. The time for the Jamstack arrived—digital consumers want responsive and adaptive content as fast as possible.

To reinforce this concept, Brian Rinaldi, developer advocate at StepZen, writes the following:

> *"What the Jamstack is continues to evolve. In just five years, we've moved from largely file-system-based Static Site Generator sites to incredibly dynamic sites driven by headless systems and APIs. It's become hard to think of a site that could not be built using the Jamstack, which is not to say that it is always the right fit. Projects like Next.js and RedwoodJS [both similar to GatsbyJS] are pushing the boundary of what the Jamstack means by including selective server-side rendering in Next.js or adding full-stack capabilities out of the box in RedwoodJS. The past of Jamstack was static sites, but the future is static first, but not static only."*

Even though we have arrived at the end of this book, we have merely scraped the surface. We have demonstrated just one simple example using one of the many versions of the various technology stacks that will together form a **Jamstack**. There are limitless combinations of headless CMSes and frontend frameworks that can be used to create many different types of products, both digital applications and also print media and PDFs. Since the frontend can be anything that sources content from an API, this architecture can be leveraged to take advantage of its pluggable nature.

The Jamstack community is constantly refining what it believes to be the best way forward, including the word *Jamstack* itself. Even during the writing of this book, the word *Jamstack* has mutated: The Jamstack community has been discussing how to capitalize the word Jamstack, so **JAMstack**, and even **JAM Stack** are present in many places.

Regarding Sanity, it is just one of many similar content management platforms. Other platforms include Contentful, Contentstack, Ghost, and Prismic, so we encourage you to learn about these as well.

Also similar to Gatsby are Next.js, Nuxt.js, Eleventy, Hugo, and Jekyll, and many more, written in programming languages such as JavaScript, Go, and Ruby, and the list is continually growing.

Lastly, similar to Netlify is Vercel, previously known as ZEIT. Also, Microsoft has now released an app service called Static Web Apps on the Azure platform, so we expect to see more options in the future.

In the next section, we will look at each technology that we have worked with in this book and discuss the community and future of each component.

The future of Sanity

Sanity Studio has evolved tremendously during the writing of this book, so the screenshots in this book reflect the latest version of the Studio user experience. Sanity will continue to focus on content as being similar to a fluid substance that fills its container, and not the container itself, which has, for many years, been the traditional web page. Knut Melvær, head of developer relations and support at Sanity, writes the following:

> *"Our position is that the future of Jamstack should embrace structured content and move away from the page approach to content modelling. That is, tooling should better allow for the reuse of content and design based on rules rather than manual editorial work."*

We are excited to see what will come as Sanity continues to grow at a very rapid pace. Next, we will look at the exciting evolution of GraphQL's tools.

The future of GraphiQL

Graphiql 2 will be the next version of Graphiql, the tool used for designing GraphQL queries. It will eventually merge features of the GraphiQL experience with the GraphQL Playground experience. Prisma, the company that developed GraphQL Playground, has donated it to the official GraphQL Foundation. Currently, the maintainer, Rikki Schulte, is focusing on reducing the need for GraphiQL or web-based IDEs entirely, by improving its language server and its reference implementation, which is the `vscode-graphql` extension, with many installations, and is preparing it to become the official GraphQL extension for the VSCode editor.

That project is located at `https://github.com/graphql/graphiql`.

The Jamstack community resources

Unfortunately, there are not enough books yet written on the Jamstack, as it is an emerging technology, but there are several that will be coming soon.

Here is a very short list of ways to learn more about the Jamstack community:

- **Websites**: There is a growing number of websites that compare *Jamstack compatible* content management systems. Here are two examples:

  CMS Comparison: `https://cms-comparison.io`

  Headless CMS: `https://headlesscms.org`

- **Podcasts**: There is a great podcast called **Jamstack Radio**. The earliest episodes talk about the origin of the word Jamstack: `https://www.heavybit.com/library/podcasts/jamstack-radio/`.

- **Courses**: This website lists Jamstack courses: `https://learnjamstack.com/courses`.

- **Chat and Discussion Groups**: There are two great Slack groups related to the Jamstack:

  The New Dynamic: `https://thenewdynamic.slack.com`

  Jamstack: `http://jamstack.slack.com`

- **Industries**: As the Jamstack works its way into many industries, we will list two of the most important industries, in terms of their importance for the future:

  Education: The Digital Humanities website at Massachusetts Institute of Technology, `https://digitalhumanities.mit.edu`, was built using the Jamstack. Also, Rollins College (`https://rollins.edu`) is recreating their website using the Jamstack. Since higher education content is largely seasonal, the Jamstack lends itself well to this need.

  Health: Jamie Bradley has developed a health-oriented application to help people with diabetes better manage their blood sugar, proving that the Jamstack is useful outside of the technology space.

  HeySugar: `https://heysugar.health`

  Create HeySugar: `https://www.sanity.io/create?template=HeySugar%2Fsanity-template-gatsby-hey-sugar`

  This shows how the Jamstack may be easily leveraged to provide life-changing solutions.

  Here is an example of how Sanity was used to build a healthcare website, showing how the Jamstack is present in the sciences: `https://www.mjhlifesciences.com`.

- **Conferences**: The most well-known conference at the time of writing is the **JamstackConf**. The Jamstack conference is held several times yearly at various locations or virtually and features speakers on a wide range of topics and also workshops. The conference URL is `https://jamstackconf.com/`.

Not only can we learn and chat with other like-minded developers, but we can actually work with code, as well. In the following section, we'll learn about how to do this.

Contributing to Jamstack projects

A great portion of the technologies used in this book are open source, so we encourage contributions to each of the platforms. It's a wonderful way to have a lasting impact on both your own future and the future of the Jamstack ecosystem, in general.

Contributing to Sanity

In this section, we'll explain how to contribute to the Sanity Studio platform.

The Sanity community

The **Sanity community** has a Slack group located at the following address: `https://sanity-io-land.slack.com`. You can receive an invitation to join by visiting `https://slack.sanity.io`. There are various channels including a channel for help, channels for announcements and beta features, and even a jobs channel. The community is rapidly growing.

Studio

Since Sanity Studio is an open source project, you too can contribute to it. The source code is located at `https://github.com/sanity-io/sanity`.

As a standard GitHub repository, it can be cloned, and a local version can be maintained. Issues can be reported, and through pull requests, a developer may request that changes become integrated into the main code base and included in the next version. In fact, the feature branch containing the future version is actually called next, so that is where pull requests should be created.

Starter kits

The starter kit that was used for this book, located at `https://sanity.io/create`, is one of a growing list of starter templates used to quickly create a Jamstack-based website. Sanity has opened the creation of starter templates to their user community.

The naming convention for these starter kits is as follows:

sanity-template-frontend-type

So, for example, `sanity-template-gatsby-blog`, means using Sanity with the Gatsby frontend to create a blog. Another example is `sanity-template-kitchen-sink`, which is used to demonstrate most of the features that Sanity has to offer. There are starter templates that use various frontend frameworks, such as Next.js, Nuxt.js, and Eleventy.

Using the basic instructions located at `https://www.sanity.io/docs/starter-templates`, we easily created `https://github.com/chrispecoraro/sanity-template-jigsaw-blog`, which uses Jigsaw, a popular **Static Site Generator (SSG)** created by Tighten, and is based on the Laravel modern PHP Framework, and the Blade templating system.

The Sanity **create** page can be called by using the following format, where `template` is a parameter and `chrispecoraro/sanity-template-jigsaw-blog` is the GitHub repository: `https://www.sanity.io/create?template=chrispecoraro/sanity-template-jigsaw-blog`.

The community templates are located at this page near the bottom: `https://www.sanity.io/create`:

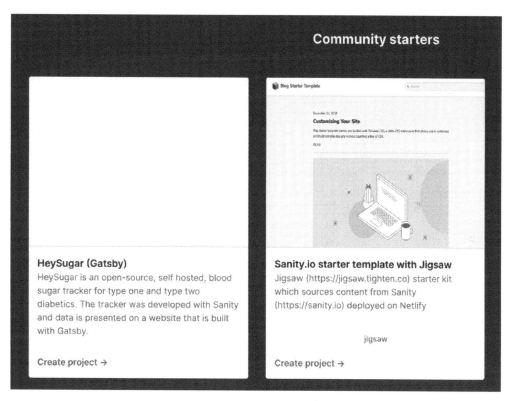

Figure 15.1 – Sanity starter kits

Migration and integration

Integrating Sanity with other code bases is easy, thanks to a set of tools available to present portable text in different usable formats, such as hyperscript and Markdown and libraries for PHP and .NET: `https://www.sanity.io/docs/presenting-block-text`.

Also, a set of tools for importing HTML content from other content management systems into Sanity may be used to convert it into a format that Sanity will use as portable text at `https://www.npmjs.com/package/@sanity/block-tools`.

Plugins

Sanity also has a series of plugins, both official and community contributed, located at `https://www.sanity.io/plugins`:

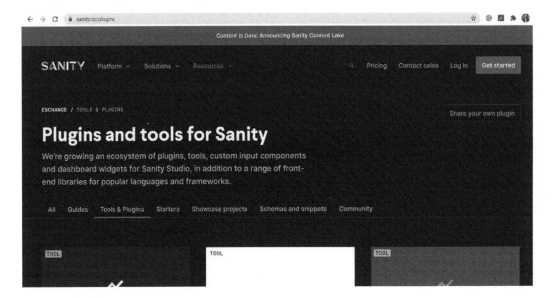

Figure 15.2 – Gatsby plugins

Plugins should be tested, uploaded as a package to `https://www.npmjs.com`, and then shared in **#I-made-this channel** in Sanity's Slack.

The future

Sanity Studio has added a feature called **presence**, which shows the document modification history, which allows users to compare any revision and revert any field.

Here is a screenshot of this new functionality:

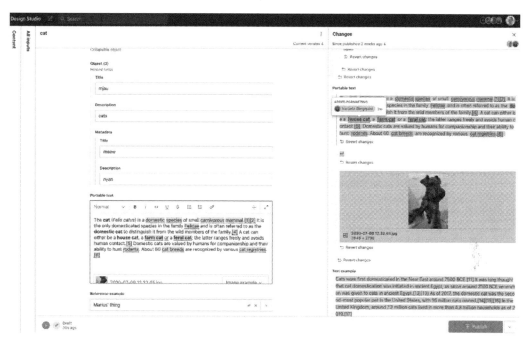

Figure 15.3 – Presence in Sanity Studio

Contributing to Gatsby

Next, we'll show how to contribute to Gatsby. Gatsby is the most open source product in this version of the Jamstack.

The Gatsby community

The Gatsby community uses several means of communication.

DEV, a software developer community, has a Gatsby community located at `https://dev.to/t/gatsby`, as well as a hashnode URL, `https://hashnode.com/n/gatsby`, and there is a Gatsby Discord located at `https://gatsby.dev/discord`, which is very full and active.

Gatsby repositories

Gatsby's GitHub URL is located at `https://github.com/gatsbyjs`.

Contributing to the Gatsby community has an added incentive: if a pull request gets accepted, the Gatsby community currently gives points that may be redeemed for swag such as a t-shirt or a water bottle.

There are many separate repositories. For example, starter themes similar to the theme used for the example in this book have names beginning with **gatsby-starter** and are located at `https://github.com/gatsbyjs/gatsby-starter-theme`.

These are good starting points to learn how Gatsby can be used with different parts of the Jamstack ecosystem.

Gatsby plugins

Gatsby plugins were discussed earlier in this book. Plugins can be created for Gatsby by the community.

Contributing to Netlify

Lastly, let's look at how to contribute to Netlify.

The Netlify community

Netlify is one of the largest parts of the Jamstack ecosystem. The Netlify community is found at `https://community.netlify.com`. The Netlify GitHub is located at `https://github.com/netlify`.

Netlify plugins

Netlify plugins, similar to the plugin that we tested in *Chapter 14, Deployment Using Netlify and Azure*, may be created and contributed following the guidance provided in the repository located at `https://github.com/netlify/plugins`.

Final thoughts

We are proud to have added this book to the Jamstack ecosystem and hope that it will be remembered as one of the first books to be released on the topic. We encourage you to add to the growing ecosystem and await contributions. Thank you immensely for having participated in our project and we wish you the best of fortune during your learning adventure and career.

Packt.com

Subscribe to our online digital library for full access to over 7,000 books and videos, as well as industry leading tools to help you plan your personal development and advance your career. For more information, please visit our website.

Why subscribe?

- Spend less time learning and more time coding with practical eBooks and Videos from over 4,000 industry professionals

- Improve your learning with Skill Plans built especially for you

- Get a free eBook or video every month

- Fully searchable for easy access to vital information

- Copy and paste, print, and bookmark content

Did you know that Packt offers eBook versions of every book published, with PDF and ePub files available? You can upgrade to the eBook version at packt.com and as a print book customer, you are entitled to a discount on the eBook copy. Get in touch with us at customercare@packtpub.com for more details.

At www.packt.com, you can also read a collection of free technical articles, sign up for a range of free newsletters, and receive exclusive discounts and offers on Packt books and eBooks.

Other Books You May Enjoy

If you enjoyed this book, you may be interested in these other books by Packt:

Drupal 9 Module Development - Third Edition

Daniel Sipos

ISBN: 978-1-80020-462-1

- Develop custom Drupal 9 modules for your applications
- Master different Drupal 9 subsystems and APIs
- Model, store, manipulate, and process data for effective data management
- Display data and content in a clean and secure way using the theme system
- Test your business logic to prevent regression
- Stay ahead of the curve and write PHP code by implementing best practices

WordPress 5 Cookbook

Rakhitha Nimesh Ratnayake

ISBN: 978-1-83898-650-6

- Install and customize WordPress themes and plugins for building websites

- Develop modern web designs without the need to write any code

- Explore the new Gutenberg content editor introduced in WordPress 5 (Bebo)

- Use the existing WordPress plugins to add custom features and monetize your website

- Improve user interaction and accessibility for your website with simple tricks

- Discover powerful techniques for maintaining and securing your websites

- Extend built-in WordPress features for advanced website management

Packt is searching for authors like you

If you're interested in becoming an author for Packt, please visit `authors.packtpub.com` and apply today. We have worked with thousands of developers and tech professionals, just like you, to help them share their insight with the global tech community. You can make a general application, apply for a specific hot topic that we are recruiting an author for, or submit your own idea.

Leave a review - let other readers know what you think

Please share your thoughts on this book with others by leaving a review on the site that you bought it from. If you purchased the book from Amazon, please leave us an honest review on this book's Amazon page. This is vital so that other potential readers can see and use your unbiased opinion to make purchasing decisions, we can understand what our customers think about our products, and our authors can see your feedback on the title that they have worked with Packt to create. It will only take a few minutes of your time, but is valuable to other potential customers, our authors, and Packt. Thank you!

Index

A

additional author
  creating 30, 31
Alexa 153
Alexa Developer Console 154
Alexa skill
  code section 168-174
  configuring, through skill
      interface 158, 159
  creating 154-158
  interface 154
  life cycle 154
  service 154
  test section 179, 180
Alexa skill, build section
  about 159
  endpoint 166
  handler, building 175178
  intent history 164
  interaction model 160-163
  invocation 160
  JSON Editor 165
  slot types 166
  utterance conflicts 164
Amazon Web Services (AWS) 146, 195

APIs, in Gatsby
  form, deploying to Netlify 140-142
  Netlify form, creating 137-140
  Netlify function, configuring 146-148
  token form, configuring in Sanity 142
  using 136
Application Programming Interfaces
      (APIs) 7, 15, 91, 102, 135, 136
articles
  adding 32
  creating 33-35
  removing 32
Asynchronous JavaScript and
      XML (Ajax) 5
Azure Static Web Apps
  continuous deployment 206-208
  creating 202-204
  deployment 201

C

camel case 43
Cascading Style Sheets (CSS) 7, 181
cloud 5
code
  cleaning up 188-190

code deployment
  preparing 187
command line
  Netlify, deploying via 200, 201
Common Gateway Interface (CGI) 3, 4
content
  modeling, with schemas 40
Content Delivery Network (CDN) 7
Content Management Systems (CMS) 4

D

digital subscriber line (DSL) 6
Document Object Model (DOM) 185
dotenv file
  about 86, 87
  client configuration 87
Drupal
  querying, with GraphQL 117, 118

E

ECMAScript 6 (ES6) 8
event.js template
  building 130-132
event schema 49, 50
example articles
  removing 32
example author
  modifying 28
existing author
  modifying 28-30

F

filesystem
  querying 118, 120
forms 4

G

Gatsby
  contributing to 219
  installing 85, 86
  project structure 82
Gatsby community
  about 219
  reference link 219
gatsby-config.js
  about 83
  structure 83
  syntax 84, 85
gatsby develop command 89
Gatsby files
  gatsby-browser.js 88
  gatsby-node.js 88
  gatsby-ssr.js 88
Gatsby folders
  public 89
  src 88
GatsbyJS
  about 9
  GraphQL 92-94
  layout modifications 182
Gatsby page components
  about 125
  building 125, 126
  modifying 125, 126
Gatsby partial components
  about 132
  building 132-134
  modifying 132-134
Gatsby Plugin Library
  about 106, 107
  advantages 107
  bug fixing 107
  improvements 107

security 107
time-saving 107
Gatsby plugins
  about 102, 220
  configuring 106
  installing 106
  Node Package Manager (npm) 102
  package, installing from npm 103, 104
  reference link 107
  searching 106, 108, 109
  semantic versioning 103
  updating 105, 106
Gatsby repositories
  about 220
  reference link 219
gatsby-source-drupal plugin
  configuring 116, 117
  Drupal, querying with
      GraphQL 117, 118
  installing 116
  querying 118, 120
gatsby-source-filesystem plugin
  configuring 109-112
  installing 109, 110
Gatsby template components
  about 126
  building 126-129
  event.js template, building 130-132
  modifying 126-129
gatsby-transformer-remark plugin
  configuring 112, 113
  content file, creating 113, 114
  filesystem, querying with
      GraphiQL 114-116
  installing 112
gigabytes (GB) 20
GraphiQL
  about 90, 94-100

filesystem, querying with 114-116
  future 214
  reference link 214
Graphiql 2 214
Graph Oriented Query (GROQ) language
  about 177
  features 58
  need for 58, 59
  querying 61, 62
  versus SQL 60
  vision, installing 59, 60
GraphQL
  about 70
  all query 72
  Drupal, querying with 117, 118
  in GatsbyJS 92-94
  reference link 70
  single-record query 73
  syntax 71, 72
  versus GROQ 73-76
GraphQL API
  deploying 71
GraphQL navigator 94-100
GraphQL playground
  basics 76-78
  query parameters 78, 79
Graph-Relational Object
      Queries (GROQ) 15
GROQ, advanced queries
  about 66
  events, selecting by venues 66
  response, formatting 67
  result, counting 67
GROQ, basic queries
  about 62
  event fields, selecting 64, 65
  events, selecting 62, 63
  non-virtual conferences, selecting 64

past events, selecting 64
relationships fields, selecting 65
upcoming events, selecting 63
virtual conferences, selecting 64

H

HTML Minify 196-198
HyperText Markup Language/Cascading
    Style Sheets (HTML/CSS) 102
HyperText Markup Language
    (HTML) 2, 3
Hypertext Preprocessor (PHP) 4
HyperText Transfer Protocol
    (HTTP) 15, 136
HyperText Transfer Protocol
    Secure (HTTPS) 8

I

integrated development
    environment (IDE) 10, 94

J

Jamstack, advantages
  about 7
  developer experience 8
  less error-prone 8
  security 8
  speed 7
Jamstack, evolution
  Asynchronous JavaScript
    and XML (Ajax) 5
  cloud 5
  Common Gateway Interface (CGI) 3, 4
  Content Management Systems (CMS) 4
  forms 4

high-speed access 6
HyperText Markup Language
    (HTML) 2, 3
JavaScript frameworks 5
server-side includes (SSI) 3
web page preprocessors 4
WordPress 5
Jamstack projects
  contributing to 216
Jamstack, software applications
  about 9
  GatsbyJS 9
  Netlify 9
  Sanity.io 9
JavaScript, APIs, and Markup (Jamstack)
  about 1, 6, 7, 212, 213
  community resources 214, 215
  evolution 2
  future 212
  installing 10
  prerequisites 10
  working with 9
JavaScript frameworks 5
JSX 82

K

kilobytes (KB) 20

L

Lerna
  using 53-56

M

megabits per second (Mbps) 6
megabytes (MB) 20

minification 196

N

namespacing 92
Netlify
  about 9, 194, 195
  contributing to 220
  deploying, via command line 200, 201
  form, deploying to 140-142
Netlify community
  about 220
  URL 220
Netlify form
  creating 137-140
Netlify function
  configuring 146-148
  submission-created.js file,
    creating 148-151
Netlify GitHub
  reference link 220
Netlify platform
  website, redeploying through 37, 38
Netlify plugins
  about 196, 220
  HTML Minify 196-198
  reference link 220
netlify.toml file
  advanced configuration,
    through 198-200
Node Package Manager (npm)
  about 10, 102
  URL 15

O

one-to-many relationship 48
one-to-one relationship 46-48

P

package.json file 104, 105
package.lock file 106
plugins, Sanity
  reference link 218
presence 218
primitive 46

R

React 82
React components
  about 124
  Gatsby page components 125
  Gatsby partial components 132
  Gatsby template components 126
  tag convention 124
  types 124
Really Simple Syndication (RSS) 106
references 46
REpresentational State Transfer
    (REST) 107

S

Sanity
  approved field, creating 142
  contributing to 216
  future 214, 218
  integration 217
  migration 218
  plugin 218
  starter kits 216, 217
  token form, configuring in 142
  URL 14
Sanity account
  setup 14

Sanity community
  about 216
  reference link 216
Sanity.io 9, 15
Sanity.io project creation
  about 15-18
  URL 15
Sanity.io project pages
  about 19
  datasets 21
  team 20
  usage 20
Sanity.io project pages, settings
  about 21
  CORS Origins 21
Sanity Manage 19
Sanity schemas
  reference link 46
Sanity Studio
  about 216
  cloning 40, 41
  folders, exploring 42
  overview 22
  reference link 216
Sanity Studio folders
  author schema 44
  exploring 42
  sanity.json file, examining 42
  schema, defining 44
  schema fields 44, 45
  schemas folder, examining 43
Sanity Studio, Navigation menu
  about 22
  Dashboard, Edit your content 23
  Dashboard, Netlify sites 23
  Dashboard, Project info 23
  Dashboard, Project users 24
  Dashboard, Recent blog posts 24

Desk 24
Desk, Authors 25
Desk, Blog post 24
Desk, Categories 25
Desk, settings 24
Sanity token
  deploying 143-146
schema fields
  about 44, 45
  types 45, 46
schema file 52
schemas
  content, modeling 40
  deploying 49, 52
  extending 49
  modifying 49
  relationships 46
schemas folder
  examining 43
  title attribute 43
  type attribute 44
schemas relationships
  one-to-one relationship 46-48
Search Engine Optimization (SEO) 106
server-side include (SSI) 3
server-side rendering (SSR) 88
Simple Mail Transfer Protocol (SMTP) 6
single-record query 73
skill interface
  about 154
  Alexa skill, configuring
    through 158, 159
skill service 154
Software-as-a-Service (SAAS) 7
Standard Query Language (SQL)
  about 212
  querying 60, 62

versus Graph Oriented Query
(GROQ) language 60
Static Site Generator (SSG) 217
submission-created.js file
creating 148-151

T

Tailwind CSS framework
about 182
event list, formatting 186, 187
event list, improving 186, 187
event proposal form,
formatting 183-185
installing 182, 183
using 183
template literal 84

U

Uniform Resource Locator
(URL) 15, 94, 117
Universally Unique Identifier (UUID) 63

V

venue schema 50, 51
venue visibility
toggling 190, 191
Vision 59
Visual Studio Code (VS Code) 10

W

web page preprocessors 4
website
name, setting 36
redeploying 35
redeploying, through Netlify
platform 37, 38
settings, modifying 35
WordPress 5

Made in United States
Orlando, FL
17 January 2022

13624539R00139